MW00618001

THE TRIUMPH OF THE REDEEMED

An Eternal Perspective that Calms Our Fears in Perilous Times

THE TRIUMPH OF THE REDEEMED

JONATHAN C. BRENTNER

DEFENDER

CRANE, MO

The Triumph of the Redeemed: An Eternal Perspective that Calms Our Fears in Perilous Times
By Jonathan C. Brentner

Defender Publishing
Crane, MO 65633
© 2021 Thomas Horn

All Rights Reserved. Published 2021.

Printed in the United States of America.

ISBN: 9781948014557

A CIP catalog record of this book is available from the Library of Congress.

Cover design by Jeffrey Mardis.

Unless otherwise indicated, Scripture quotations are from The ESV® Bible (The Holy Bible, English Standard Version®), copyright © 2001 by Crossway, a publishing ministry of Good News Publishers. Used by permission. All rights reserved.

I dedicate this book to my wonderful wife Ruth
for her kindness, loving support, encouragement,
and tireless editing, and helpful feedback
as I wrote this book.

Contents

Section Four

The Triumph of the Redeemed

Acknowledgments

My study during the past several years has given me a deeper appreciation for the Bible professors who not only taught me God's Word, but who also prepared me for a lifetime of learning.

First, I want to acknowledge a couple of wonderful professors at John Brown University during my time of study there from 1971 to 1975:

- Dr. James Walters
- Dr. Andrew Bowling

I'm also grateful for my excellent and wonderful professors at Talbot Theological Seminary, 1975–1978, who established a firm foundation within me for premillennialism and the pre-Tribulation Rapture:

- Dr. Richard Rigsby
- Dr. Robert Saucy
- Dr. Robert Thomas
- Dr. Henry Holloman
- Dr. Charles Fienberg

I owe a deep debt of gratitude to all these godly and wise men, along with Dr. Louis Talbot, whom I never had the pleasure of meeting.

I especially want acknowledge Angie Peters, who edited the manuscript of this book. Her excellent work made it more readable and easier to understand.

Introduction

Is Biblical Prophecy Relevant to Our Everyday Lives?

> As long as the resurrected universe remains either undesirable or unimaginable, Satan succeeds in sabotaging our love for Heaven.
>
> ~Randy Alcorn, *Heaven*[1]

One evening during our weekly small group gathering, dear friends shared a video of their delightful granddaughter who had died a year earlier. Doctors had discovered a malignant tumor in her abdomen the day after her first birthday, and for over a year she endured surgeries, chemotherapy, and lengthy hospital stays as the cancer relentlessly overwhelmed her tiny body. On October 24, 2015, this precious girl went home to be with Jesus.

As we watched the story of her brief life unfold before us, we shared in the grief of her grandparents. Tears came to the eyes of many of us. We couldn't understand why her stay on earth had ended so soon, but we knew that cancer wasn't the end of her story. She now dwells with the Lord in heaven, where her bright smile continues to bring joy to those around her.

For her grandparents, the promises in Scripture regarding eternity are anything but dry theology; they represent comfort and survival when the winds of grief sweep over them. Our friends experienced much sorrow watching their granddaughter suffer and finally succumb to cancer. Now they look forward to seeing her smile, hearing her laugh, and feeling her arms wrap around them when they reunite with her in heaven one day.

The words of Revelation 21:4 kept coming to my mind that evening:

> He will wipe away every tear from their eyes, and death shall be no more, neither shall there be mourning, nor crying, nor pain anymore, for the former things have passed away.

What a contrast those words provide to the sorrow and pain we so often experience in this life!

Who can understand why so many children today incur the grievous affliction of cancer? How can we cope with such tragedies apart from the hope of a better day when the Lord will make all things new and forever eliminate pain, sorrow, cancer, and death?

Scripture provides many promises of eternity that both comfort and encourage our hearts during times of despair. On this side of heaven, we will experience disappointments, loss, and tear-filled nights. The Bible, however, promises believers a much better day, one in which we will experience Christ's resurrection life, reign with Him in His kingdom, and forever share in His triumph over sin and death during the eternal state described in Revelation chapters 21 and 22.

My Purpose for Writing

My purpose for writing this book is to show how the specifics of Bible prophecy intersect with our daily lives in a way that calms our fears and encourages our hearts during the perilous times in which we live. The "blessed hope" of the gospel points us to the glorious moment when eternity begins for all who know the Savior (Titus 2:11–14). However, few believers today focus on the joy of meeting Jesus in the air. Instead, they endure affliction and heartaches with a shortsighted perspective that fails to look beyond their earthly existence.

My desire for writing *The Triumph of the Redeemed* is to reconnect the gospel with Jesus' imminent appearing in a way that breathes hope into your heart, regardless of what you face today or in the future.

Perhaps you're reading this book with a basic understanding of scriptural teachings regarding the Rapture, the Second Coming, and the Millennium, yet you too often forget about the blissful future that's ahead. You may find it difficult to link what you believe about eternity with temporal issues like your relationship woes, overdue bills, illnesses, layoffs, and anxieties that come from living in a lawless world that grows more chaotic and violent by the day.

Maybe you're not very familiar with Bible prophecy, yet you long for reassurance regarding what lies ahead as the turmoil increases. As your worries escalate, you wonder if a better day exists. Is there really a "happily ever after"? Does the Bible provide any reassurance concerning the dark days ahead?

You might think it's foolish to watch for Jesus' appearing. It's been two thousand years since He told us He would return; why should we expect Him to appear anytime soon? Is He really coming again? How can we be certain of what the Bible says about the future?

If you can relate to any of these scenarios or questions, *The Triumph of the Redeemed* is for you!

God designed the study of future things, what theologians refer to as "eschatology," to encourage us *each day* as we step out of bed. Regardless of the messiness of our lives or the discouraging news reports that greet us each morning, an unwavering focus on the joys ahead in eternity injects needed assurance into our hearts and relieves anxieties regarding the future.

Why the Loss of Excitement?

"If there's really so much to look forward to in eternity," you might also ask, "why have so many believers lost their eagerness for it? Why do even seasoned students of prophecy at times lose their focus on our Lord's appearing and their future reign with Him?"

I believe this happens for many reasons:

The busyness of life: It's easy to live as though this temporal world is all we have. We get up, eat, go to work, return home, eat again, watch TV, and go to bed. We do a hundred different things throughout the day that focus our attention solely on the things of this existence with the result that we soon forget about eternity. Even if we spend time studying the Word and praying each morning, we soon find that the all-consuming activities of our days redirect our thoughts to temporal concerns.

I'm not saying we should concentrate on heaven all day long; if we did, we might not get anything done at work or at home! Yet we often go about our routines oblivious to the joys Jesus has planned for us after this life.

We live as though we have no hope beyond the grave, despite what we claim to believe.

Misconceptions about heaven: When it comes to heaven, misconceptions abound. How often have we seen depictions of solitary men and women sitting on clouds, strumming harps? Who would even look forward to such a dull existence? Not me!

Some believers imagine that heaven will be an unending worship service. Of course, we will sing God's praises throughout eternity, but the Lord has so much more in store for us once we reach the brighter shore.

I love the movie *It's a Wonderful Life*, but someday we will be far more than aspiring angels jumping into icy waters to earn our wings. In fact, Scripture not only *does not* say we'll *become* angels, but it says that we will "*judge* angels" (1 Corinthians 6:3). I'm not sure of all that implies, but it certainly distinguishes us from them.

Perhaps the most popular myth regarding heaven is that it will be boring. Nothing could be farther from the truth; this is the greatest delusion of all!

Randy Alcorn, in his wonderful book, *Heaven*, addresses this fallacy:

> Our belief that Heaven will be boring betrays a heresy—that God is boring. There's no greater nonsense. Our desire for pleasure and the experience of joy come directly from God's hand. He made our taste buds, adrenaline, sex drives, and the nerve endings that convey pleasure to our brains. Likewise, our imaginations and our capacity for joy and exhilaration were made by the very God we accuse of being boring. Are we so arrogant as to imagine that human beings came up with the idea of having fun?[2]

In Psalm 16:11, David confirms this upbeat view of eternity with these words:

> In your presence there is fullness of joy; at your right hand are pleasures forevermore.

"I've heard that before": Back in the 1960s and 1970s, eschatology became a hot topic. Many churches emphasized the soon return of Jesus. I remember the week televangelist Jack Van Impe came to my church to teach about prophecy. After hearing his words, I felt the excitement of waiting for the Lord's imminent appearing.

Many decades, however, have passed since then. Large numbers of believers have lost their expectancy of Jesus' return, and they often respond with "I've heard that before" to those telling them to watch for it. Having anticipated the Rapture for five decades, I understand the sentiment that finds it more than a little challenging to remain focused on that stunning event.

Yet, as we see the circumstances and events described in biblical prophecy coming to life before our eyes today at an ever-accelerating pace, if there was ever a time to be mindful of eternal matters, it's now! An abundance of converging signs point to the soon beginning of the Tribulation and thus to Jesus' imminent return for His Church, an event that will happen before the onset of the terrible time of the Lord's wrath upon the earth.

Don't let the sentiment behind "I've heard that before" take your focus away from the glorious prize that awaits you when Jesus comes for us!

Silence in the pulpits: Rather than increase their focus on Jesus' return as the day approaches, many pastors either remain quiet about our hope or they reject biblical teaching about it. Such silence not only takes the eyes of those in the pews (or chairs) off the Lord's return, but it also deadens their expectation of it. How can the saints look forward to something they seldom or perhaps never hear about?

When pastors mention life beyond the grave, the subject often comes across as such a fleeting and lifeless allusion that those in the congregation forget about it by the end of the sermon. Such lackluster mentions of our gospel hope don't stir our hearts or relieve our anxieties for the week ahead.

Teaching that lacks a biblical, two-world perspective: When pastors and church leaders don't present instruction based on a biblical, two-world perspective (2 Corinthians 4:17–18), they unwittingly make goals such as happy marriages, good parenting, and wise financial planning the ultimate hope of believers.

Of course, biblically centered teaching on such matters is *essential.* However, without a two-world outlook integrated into such instruction, these issues easily become all-consuming. As a result, believers put all their efforts into becoming "better Christians" and soon forget about forever.

Problems arise when the saints (believers) place their *ultimate* hopes on temporal outcomes wherein many factors, including sinful choices, negatively impact the results they so greatly desire. Children rebel, wives leave husbands and vice versa, finances fall apart, and tragedies often turns lives upside down.

What's left when believers do their best to adhere to biblically sound principles, yet everything falls apart, and they end up alone to pick up the broken pieces?

I know of such turmoil; *it happened to me.*

The New Testament teaches us to expect difficult times (James 1:2–3; 1 Peter 1:6; 4:12–13). The Lord promises paradise once He comes for us—but not now. We set ourselves up for disappointment if we define anything in this life as our *ultimate* hope, even if it's scriptural, desirable, praiseworthy, good, or wholesome.

I'm not at all saying that we fail to enjoy the things of this life and the many blessings God sends our way. A two-world outlook doesn't mean that we fail to dream, set goals, or plan wisely for our future. It does, however, teach us to place our ultimate aspirations on eternal realities versus the fleeting matters of this life.

Why Do the Specifics Matter?

"What's the big deal?" you might ask. "As long as I believe in my future resurrection from the dead and possess a general understanding of heaven, what difference does it make what I believe about the Rapture, the Tribulation, Christ's Second Coming, or the Millennium?"

The danger of ignoring these specifics is this: Instead of eagerly waiting for Jesus' appearing, our fondest desires naturally shift to matters in this life—to *our* plans for *our* future. Momentary concerns soon consume our focus, and thoughts of Jesus' imminent return rarely, if ever, enter our minds. Paul David Tripp describes this malady as "modern evangelical schizophrenia," which he describes in this way:

> It is the fact that we declare that we believe in forever, yet live as if this is all there is. This functional contradiction between our belief system and our daily living cannot work. Here's why.
>
> First, you cannot make sense out of the Christian life without eternity. This is the whole argument of 1 Corinthians 15....
>
> Second, you and I have been hardwired for eternity. Ecclesiastes 3:11 declares that God has placed eternity in every person's heart. That means that everyone hungers for paradise. No one is satisfied with things the way they are.[3]

It's the details of our everlasting hope that enable us to put the ups and downs of our lives as well as chaotic world events into a sound biblical prophetic framework that offers assurance of God's unfailing sovereignty over all that concerns us. These specifics redirect our attention to the joys ahead in paradise during times when life doesn't make sense, or when all seems lost.

The divorce of the Rapture from the message of the gospel has resulted in a near blackout of teaching about our "blessed hope" (Titus 2:11–14). This negatively affects new believers as well as seasoned saints, as it leaves them ill-prepared to live in a fear-ridden society. In addition, this neglect, or even denial, of Bible prophecy provides no context into which a follower of Jesus can place the violence and lawlessness of our day or the push for a New World Order or what the World Economic Forum calls the "Great Reset."

I read that one teacher stated our belief in a literal interpretation of the book of Revelation creates fear among the faithful. However, just the opposite is true. A proper understanding of the end-time events prophesied in Scripture enables us to face the headlines of our day without giving into despair or hopelessness.

It's a focus on the joy that lies ahead that calms our hearts amid our daily struggles as well as when reports of disconcerting world events fill our newsfeeds. This mindset enables us to put to today's widespread wickedness and thwarting of justice into a perspective that brings inner peace. *The biblical teachings regarding our future are where we find relief from the anxious thoughts that so easily creep into our minds during these perilous times.*

It takes much more than just a cursory head knowledge of our eternal hope to survive in this hostile world where deception reigns in the minds of so many and our adversary seeks to destroy us in whatever way he can. We must hold on to the specifics of our hope like we would hold on to a raft going through wild rapids on a river.

Section One

The Two-World Perspective of the Gospel

What is it about an eternal perspective that reassures us despite the perilous times in which we live? Christian author John Eldredge sums up the ingredient that is so often lacking in our attempts to live out the hope of the gospel:

> Given the suffocating, pathological unbelief and anti-romanticism of our post-postmodern culture, you are going to have to make very conscious choices to take hold of this hope [the promised kingdom]. Allowance—the renewal of all things might be true—is not taking hold. Acceptance—okay, I think it is—is not taking hold. We need to grab this hope like we would hug the person in front of us if we were passengers on a wild motorcycle ride; we need to "take hold" like you do at the top of a ladder when you suddenly think you are falling. Seize is a far better description; we need to seize this hope.[4]

Although Eldredge states our need of an eternal perspective far more eloquently than I can, the point remains the same: We need so much more than a passive understanding of our "promised kingdom." A simple awareness of the facts about biblical prophecy doesn't suffice when the storms of life burst through our door. In order to withstand such assaults, we must grab hold of our expectation of a joyous eternity and live as though it's more valuable than any temporal treasure, experience, or outcome. That's the essence of a biblical, two-world perspective.

It's not as though we can lose our eternal inheritance as saints; Scripture assures us that we cannot lose our salvation. However, we too often wander down shortsighted paths by overlooking the significance of what lies ahead in paradise and what it means for the afflictions and disappointments that so often greet us.

I discovered the necessity of maintaining a firm grasp on a two-world perspective the hard way. Although I *knew* biblical prophecy and *loved* to preach about it as a young pastor, I didn't value eternal joy above my temporal goals. When my life fell apart, I grasped for fleeting earthly aspirations rather than seize the Lord's promise of His appearing and of my future reign with Him in His kingdom.

A biblically sound, two-world outlook on life wouldn't have enabled me to avoid the disastrous circumstances that turned my world upside down and inside out, but it would have alleviated the painful despair and anxieties that lingered for many years. I struggled with PTSD (post-traumatic stress disorder) far longer than necessary because of my temporal, earthbound perspective.

It wasn't until I learned to *value* my hope of glory over my fleeting ambitions for this life that my PTSD symptoms began to wane and eventually disappear—but I'm getting ahead of myself. Before recounting my painful personal experiences, I'll answer this question: What is a biblical, two-world perspective?

1

The Greater Weight of Eternity

> If we consider the unblushing promises of reward and the staggering nature of the rewards promised in the Gospels, it would seem that our Lord finds our desires not too strong, but too weak. We are half-hearted creatures, fooling about with drink and sex and ambition when infinite joy is offered us, like an ignorant child who wants to go on making mud pies in a slum because he cannot imagine what is meant by the offer of a holiday at the sea. We are far too easily pleased.
>
> -C.S. Lewis, "The Weight of Glory" sermon

Imagine you're living from paycheck to paycheck, barely able to survive while working at a job you hate (maybe a few of you already identify with this picture). Add to this scenario the absolute certainty that, in one year's time, you will inherit $200 million, provided you stay with your current employment for the entire year. (I know I may have lost *all* of you with that proposition.)

What would occupy your thoughts as you drive to work each day? Wouldn't the promise of your future inheritance change how you respond to missed promotions at work, mounting bills, or any number of other financial woes? Of course it would!

The prospect of great wealth would likely make a dramatic difference in how you would respond to all the major and minor irritations in your lives. Traffic jams on the way to work might seem far less frustrating, as would long checkout lines at stores. An hour probably wouldn't go by without thoughts of how you would enjoy your enormous fortune. The assurance of your future prosperity would change your perspective about everything.

The spiritual reality for every follower of Jesus actually exceeds the expected wealth in the above illustration; we will forever enjoy our heavenly inheritance. Is that not worth more than any temporary earthly treasure? Paul said this in Romans 8:18:

> For I consider that the sufferings of this present time are not worth comparing with the glory that is to be revealed to us.

The apostle says the wonders ahead for us in eternity *far outweigh* all our current troubles and misfortunes.

Picture a balance scale. On one side, you see the pan weighed down with the splendors waiting for you in eternity, while on the other side, you see the vessel filled with all the past difficulties and heartbreaks you've experienced. Now envision the joy ahead for you in paradise weighing down the pan on that side to the extreme. No amount of added suffering from this life placed in the tray on the other side changes the balance in even the slightest way. The "glory" side of the scale remains fully weighted down in favor of eternity—regardless of the sorrows added to the temporal side.

We naturally regard our earthly troubles as far outweighing the thrills ahead in heaven, but just the opposite is true. In the quote at the beginning of this chapter, British writer and theologian C. S. Lewis referred to the "staggering nature of the rewards promised in the Gospels." There's no way to compare the surpassing wonders and pleasures ahead with even the best things this life offers.

Paul's Remarkable Two-World Perspective

Remarkably, Paul maintained his Romans 8:18 comparison of glory versus earthly trauma despite tremendous suffering. In 2 Corinthians 11:24–28, he shared what he endured as an apostle:

> Five times I received at the hands of the Jews the forty lashes less one. Three times I was beaten with rods. Once I was stoned. Three times I was shipwrecked; a night and a day I was adrift at sea; on frequent journeys, in danger from rivers, danger from robbers, danger from my own people, danger from Gentiles, danger in the city, danger in the wilderness, danger at sea, danger from false brothers; in toil and hardship, through many a sleepless night, in hunger and thirst, often without food, in cold and exposure. And, apart from other things, there is the daily pressure on me of my anxiety for all the churches.

All the persecution, adversities, and dangers listed in the above text did not even tip the balance away from the glories of eternity for Paul. In 2 Corinthians 4:17–18, he said:

> For this light momentary affliction is preparing for us an eternal weight of glory beyond all comparison, as we look not to the things that are seen but to the things that are unseen. For the things that are seen are transient, but the things that are unseen are eternal.

Although we regard Paul's sufferings as extreme and far, far above normal, the apostle referred to them as "light momentary affliction." How could he possibly view them in such a way apart from a biblical two-world perspective, one with the scale heavily favoring the glories ahead in eternity?

While not discounting the severity of his persecutions and abundant hardships, Paul placed a superior worth, a greater value, on matters with eternal significance. He compared his many afflictions with the joys of paradise, not with the experiences of the guy seated in the chair next to him at church or the many success stories he heard from other saints (or that he read about on social media).

The Importance of a Two-World Outlook

Such an outlook is not just something beneficial for spiritual giants like the Apostle Paul; it's *necessary* for us as well. In his book *Hot Tub Religion*, J. I. Packer blames the current ineffectiveness of the church on the loss of a two-world perspective among followers of Jesus.[5] He said:

> What Paul and John assumed, both from their own experience and from their God-taught understanding of divine grace, was that the reality of redeeming love and the certainty of heaven would so thrill believers' hearts that they would think about these things all the time.[6]

As believers, we place way too much importance on this life and far too little on what's to come. As a result of such a misguided value assessment, our ultimate goals switch to temporal concerns. We soon discover that such a focus does little to lift our hearts above the day-to-day drudgery or enable us to look beyond the heartaches we endure.

During the time I worked on this book, the shooting at the church in Sutherland Springs, Texas, occurred. I can't begin to imagine the horror of being inside that church as the gunman shot helpless churchgoers and small children. The grief of the families who lost loved ones that day will linger for an exceptionally long time.

But I know that my loving Savior is able to comfort His children in even the worst of tragedies. The Lord will someday wipe away all tears (Revelation 21:4), and I believe the wonders and joys of eternity will surpass *even* the horrible and gut-wrenching memories of those in that Texas church.

Before diving into the biblical foundation of our hope of eternity in paradise, I will share the painful experiences that led to my battle with PTSD as well as the rugged path of my recovery from this disorder. My story illustrates the danger of a one-world perspective that values temporal outcomes over the forever joy that lies ahead for all of us who know Jesus as Savior. It also demonstrates why the future hope of the gospel must resonate in our hearts so that we value it above all our earthly ambitions.

2

It Was 4 A.M.

> We were created to live in a forever relationship with a forever God forever. We were designed to live based on a long view of life. We were made to live with one eye on now and one eye on eternity. You and I simply cannot live as we were put together without forever.
>
> ~Paul David Tripp, *New Morning Mercies*[7]

It was 4 a.m. and I remained seated on the ground with my back leaning against the outside wall of a church. Overwhelmed with sorrow from recent events, tears flowed down my cheeks as they had for most of the past six hours. After a long night of crying out to the Lord for deliverance, I felt alone in my grief. Where was God when the walls caved in on me? Didn't He care about my turmoil and pain?

Five years earlier, I had begun my ministry at this church with great excitement. I absolutely loved being a pastor and had plans, goals, and a determination to accomplish great things for the Lord. How had my dreams turned into a nightmare of epic proportions?

Opposition at Church

The dreadful chain of events had started a few years earlier, when a few men in my church approached me with a request that I add more application to my sermons, which I attempted to do. Their appeals, however, soon morphed into strong opposition as they continued to find fault with me, my ministry, and seemingly everything I did. The harder I tried to satisfy their demands, the more mistakes I made, and their disapproval of my ministry grew.

Their confrontations continued. "You're not blessing people," they told me. "If you did, our church would be growing." Rather than partnering with me in reaching out to the community, however, they remained on sidelines, all too happy to criticize me when I didn't produce results indicating what they considered to be a "successful ministry."

One of the older women in the church voiced her disapproval of me with words that I sometimes hear in my mind even decades later: "Your ministry is a joke!" She repeated this accusation many times after evening services, making sure everyone heard her stinging words. Some defended me, but that didn't deter her from loudly repeating her opinion before she eventually left the church. I talked with her on many occasions about the issue, but it didn't stop her verbal assaults.

The opposition at church added financial distress to my predicament, as some stopped giving tithes at the insistence of those who believed I was failing as a pastor. This intensified the pressure I felt to make things happen (never a good motivation, to say the least). The harder I tried, the more mistakes I made.

The financial woes at church added considerable stress to an already-troubled situation at home. My wife had earlier fallen into a depression. I didn't understand what was happening or why she had become so angry with me in such a short period of time; it soon became clear that we *both* needed help.

We went for counseling, but that didn't bring healing to our relationship or provide meaningful relief for my wife. Our marriage continued to deteriorate despite our time with the therapist.

As things worsened on both fronts, I felt like a ball in a pinball machine ricocheting between infuriated outbursts at home and hostility at the church. As the clanging of each bounce grew louder, I became increasingly fearful for my future. I sensed intense disapproval as I preached on Sundays, and I wondered how an out-of-work and perhaps divorced pastor could find a job, or even survive.

Before they left the church, the couple leading the opposition to my ministry requested a meeting. They didn't ask me directly, but did so through a mutual friend. Because of their previous harshness with me, I was hesitant to get together with them. I agreed to, however, after the friend assured me that they wanted to resolve our differences in a peaceful manner. *Such was not the case!*

That evening, I listened as they spent a full hour denouncing *everything* I had done as a pastor. They listed my shortcomings with painstaking detail. They said I had failed to bless people on Sundays, and they demanded that I ask others in the church where they received their "blessings." It was my task to bless people on Sundays, they said, and I had not done so.

I could tell from their confrontational demeanor that any attempt to defend myself would surely result in further contempt. I glanced at my watch once during the meeting, and even that drew a mean and degrading response.

Were they wrong about all their accusations? No. The tone of their attack, however, left no room for reconciliation or any meaningful conversation regarding a path forward. They wanted someone besides me to lead the church; nothing I might have said would have changed their minds.

I felt devastated, to say the least.

Later that night I went for a long walk. This was but one of many middle-of-the-night treks I spent crying out to the Lord as I sought strength and comfort for my circumstances.

I remember walking by the home of another pastor I knew. I saw a light shining through a window and thought about seeking his counsel, but decided not to knock on his door. I'm not sure why I passed by; perhaps I dreaded letting him and others who might be with him see me in such a broken state, barely able to express my grief.

I needed help, but remained hesitant to let others into my world. Nothing in my training or background had prepared me for such passionate hostility at home as well as from those at the church.

I felt weak and battered—not a good combination for a husband or a pastor. In my distressed state, I reached the point where I believed I *deserved* the scathing anger from my wife at home and the indignant opposition from the people at church. I blamed myself for everything that had gone wrong: I could have been a better husband at home; I could have been a better pastor.

Although several people remained supportive of my ministry, it wasn't enough to make ends meet when my antagonists left. So, I took a nighttime job in a local factory while continuing to serve as a pastor. A severe injury to my hand one night resulted in a trip to the emergency room and skin-graft surgery the following week.

The combination of working thirty-two hours a week while preparing two sermons a week and keeping up with other pastoral duties added to the tensions at home. As the pressures mounted, I resigned as pastor.

Betrayal!

One of the brighter aspects of my time at the church was a friend who came to my office at times to encourage me as the opposition toward me had grown. Our bond became stronger as we worked on cars and attended sporting events together. I regarded him as a close friend and ally. I saw no reason to doubt my trust in him.

After I resigned from my position at the church, my friend's demeanor toward me changed; he became distant and appeared to feel guilt-stricken when he was around me. Several weeks later, I learned why.

He and my wife had been romantically involved for the previous three years. The news sent me into a state of shock much like when one discovers that a beloved family member has died. It took me weeks to fully comprehend the news.

I desperately longed for an advocate during this time. I needed someone to stand alongside me. The one person to whom I poured out my heart never called back, not even once. The turmoil was much more than I could bear; I felt more isolated than ever.

Regrettably, I didn't reach out to the members of my extended family until much later. They surely would have rushed to my side if I had done so, as they did when I finally told them what had happened.

My disappointment with God kept me from falling on my knees to seek His help and wisdom. Not only that, but, because of my reliance on myself, I kept the fear and anger that arose from this time and the years that followed locked inside; that proved to be a *huge* mistake.

One Night in the Garage

My emotional distress following the news of the betrayal was much more excruciating than any physical hurt I had ever experienced; not even the severe pain of the hand injury at the factory compared with the internal agony that gnawed at my soul night and day.

Thoughts of suicide entered my mind. *I did not want to die,* but I longed for an escape from the intense anguish inside me that I believed would never end.

So, one night, I walked into our garage with the intent of ending my life—but I suddenly seemed to be paralyzed. I couldn't even touch my car, let alone get inside it. Thoughts of the biblical account of Balaam popped into my mind; I remembered how an angel stopped his donkey as he traveled to curse the Israelites. I soon realized the Lord had frozen my movement; I could only return to the entrance of the garage. Once there, I felt Him push me out of the door, perhaps to ensure that I would never forget His intervention that night.

Despite Jesus' unmistakable deliverance of my life in the garage, I struggled. I went out often for many long walks late at night to pray or sometimes just to rehearse my grief with the Lord.

It was 4 a.m., and I knew I would never again be a pastor. Who would want a divorced man to lead their church? Had my seminary training been all for nothing? How could the Lord use me after all my many failures? I didn't believe He would even want to.

What was next for me? Was I destined to work forever in a dark, dingy factory where memories of my hand injury haunted me each time I walked into the building? What kind of future did I have? Where could I go?

I wanted to run far, far away from the Lord, His people, the church, and from all that life seemed to be. Looking back, I realize it was my absolute confidence in Jesus' resurrection that kept me from abandoning my faith. I knew beyond a doubt that Christ's words were true. However, despite my unwavering faith, my anger toward the Lord continued.

Rather than look forward to what the Lord might have planned for me, I allowed fear to replace hope, I embraced my troubles rather than the Lord's love for me, and I chose my solutions over seeking God's paths. Despite loving to teach about prophecy as a pastor, I responded to my calamities as though this world was my final home, and I soon became absorbed with achieving new goals for this life.

I had lost sight of forever.

Since that long, tearful night I spent beside the wall of the church,

I've learned it's not enough just to know *about* the Lord's return and the joys of heaven. The specifics of eternity must *seize* my heart and become the lens through which I see all of life if they are to bring consolation amid seemingly endless adversity.

We Have So Much More Than the Moment

Even as I write this chapter decades later, I feel a tug on my heart to ignore the joys of eternity and look again to the moment for purpose and meaning.

Paul David Tripp aptly describes this disconnect we so often feel:

> It is an item on each of our theological outlines, but we don't live as though we believe it. We all say that we believe that this is not all there is. We say we believe that there is life after this one ends. Our formal theology contains the fact of a new heaven and a new earth to come. But we tend to live with the anxiety and drivenness that come when we believe that all we have is this moment.[8]

As believers, we truly have so much more than this "moment," the occasions that make up our lifespan that passes by oh so quickly. God's loving purpose in saving us isn't only to keep us from hell, but to shower us with "the immeasurable riches of His grace in kindness toward us" throughout all eternity (Ephesians 2:7). The purpose of learning about our future with Jesus is to draw our attention away from the nonstop "drivenness" and futility of the moment to the endless joys ahead for us once this life ends.

It doesn't take a concerted effort of searching through the Bible to find the details of our joyous hope; they're within easy reach of anyone seeking relief from the "drivenness" of the moment. The Bible includes more than two thousand verses that refer to the Second Coming; Jesus referred to His return to earth twenty-one times. Most books in the New Testament point to Jesus' future appearing, His return for us, in some way.

When I look back, I wonder why I became so captivated with my earthly goals. Why didn't I trust God's love for me as His child or allow my hope to bring light into the circumstances that suddenly turned dark and daunting?

Although I didn't realize it at the time, I saw myself first as a pastor and second as a dear child of God bound for a glorious eternity. Because of my absorption with my temporal role and aspirations, I panicked (to put it mildly) when others threatened them. Instead of resting in my identity as a born-again child of God bound for the joys of an eternal paradise, I labored in my own strength to regain a respectable life.

As a result of the lingering self-absorption and attempts to make life work in the moment apart from a reliance on the Lord, my path to healing was not quick, nor did it follow a straight line; it more often resembled the route of a hockey puck slapped across the ice several times before reaching the goal.

3

PTSD, a Song, and the Broken Path to Healing

> It becomes us to spend this life only as a journey toward heaven…to which we should subordinate all other concerns of life. Why should we labor for or set our hearts on anything else, but that which is our proper end and true happiness?
>
> ~Jonathan Edwards, from *Jonathan Edwards: Basic Writings*[9]

As I looked for a job in the months following my resignation from the church, I discovered my seminary training and pastoral experience did little to impress potential employers. One voiced the opinion that I would likely return to the pastorate someday and he was thus reluctant to train me for an open internship.

As my prospects of finding another vocation faded, I returned to school. I spent months studying for the Graduate Management Admission Test (GMAT), for which I needed acceptable scores, particularly in math, to gain entrance into the MBA program at the University of Iowa. After achieving the needed exam results on my first attempt, I began graduate school.

I found a job at a nearby computer processing company that enabled me to work evenings while attending classes during the day. During my MBA studies, I emphasized accounting and finance, which proved to be a natural fit, and I did quite well in my studies. My success in obtaining an MBA boosted my self-confidence as I focused on the better days ahead. I assumed that my nightmarish past was forever behind me—but that wasn't the case.

Through a series of promotions at work, I moved up from a position as a second-shift data entry operator to a senior financial analyst. I found surprising enjoyment in being a number-cruncher and loved my new career of managing the finances for various government contracts held by my employer.

I traveled to Washington, DC, on several occasions as the result of my new role in the company. The best part of these trips was getting to be a tourist during the evenings. I went for long runs on the National Mall as I took in the sights of our beautiful capital city. I loved running by the symbols of my nation's heritage and history.

My walk with the Lord deepened during this time; I felt closer to Him than I had in many years. A key turning point came during a long run, when Jesus caught up with me and I surrendered my future to Him anew. I submitted to whatever He had for me in the months and years ahead. I finally recognized the futility of my past strivings.

I continued to write adult Sunday school curriculum for Christian publisher David C. Cook, something I began doing during my final year as a pastor and that I continue to do now. This provided welcome opportunities to use my Bible training as well as to minister to others.

A short passage from the Psalms became a treasured source of encouragement during the times I struggled with insufficient finances and loneliness. I wrote out these verses, along with Psalm 27:13–14, and put them in front of me at work:

> You have made me see many troubles and calamities
> will revive me again;
> from the depths of the earth
> you will bring me up again.
> You will increase my greatness
> and comfort me again. (Psalm 71:20–21)

During this time of spiritual renewal and much outward success, I remained unaware of the powerful anxieties that raged below the surface of my consciousness waiting for an opportunity to ambush me and plunge me into the darkness of unrelenting anxiety. The fears and anguish that I had locked away years ago hadn't dissipated, as I mistakenly thought, but had remained just as strong, waiting for a prompting to reemerge and again submerge my life in turmoil and pain.

The Perfect Storm

Many years later, I met a woman whom I thought was the answer to my loneliness. *She was not.* Our marriage got off to a rocky start and never recovered. My wife's growing discontentment with me caused a rapid downward spiral of panic inside me, which added considerable strife in our relationship.

When my counselor diagnosed my symptoms as PTSD, he said my frequent episodes of panic attacks stemmed from unresolved fears from my past, especially during the tumultuous years of my second pastorate and first marriage. Remarriage and the problems that soon surfaced reopened old wounds buried deep inside. The renewed conflict of my second marriage triggered many unresolved anxieties from my past.

It was the perfect storm. I came into the marriage with deeply buried fears. My wife entered with high expectations due to sorrows from her previous marriage. My struggles shattered her dreams for the marriage; her angry response to my issues and continued verbal abuse inflamed my PTSD symptoms. Neither of us could break free from the decline that accelerated as our frustrations with each other intensified.

Terrors in the Night

At times, my bouts with anxiety sprang up out of nowhere. I remember being remarkably peaceful one night as I fell asleep. Then, at 3 a.m., I woke up feeling overwhelmed and in a state of absolute panic. What was happening to me? How could I fall into such great fear apart from any conscious worry or perceived threat? How did my calmness suddenly morph into deep, dark terror?

On that occasion, I battled the panic attack by quoting Scripture and praying for an hour before I again sensed the Lord's peace in my heart. I recall writing in my journal that this spiritual battle was a "long bloody fight." From that point forward, I recognized the devil's role in the middle-of-the-night attacks that continued to come my way during the next several years.

A couple of years into our marriage, my wife talked to a real estate agent without my knowledge about selling our home with the goal that we would go our separate ways after the sale. Although I was quite distressed when she told me about her inquiry, I remained opposed to a separation. I dreaded the shame of having another failed marriage even more than I did the ongoing emotional and verbal abuse that many around us recognized, but didn't bring up until after our separation. I wondered why those in our Bible study group hadn't talked to me earlier about what they had witnessed.

Several months later, however, I agreed to my wife's terms: We would put our home up for sale, separate, and each purchase new houses. I saw no other choice at the time than to go along with her demands; she showed no sign of relenting from her desire to be free from me.

One week before I moved out, I attended a Steve Green concert. As I walked into the auditorium that evening, *I thought my life was over.* Thoughts of my failures as a pastor and as a husband plagued me. My future looked bleak at best; I had accepted the devil's lie that my circumstances would remain dire for the remainder of my life and that God no longer had a purpose for me.

A Song Restores My Focus on Eternity

I will never forget how the Lord spoke to me that night at the concert. As Steve Green introduced his latest song at that time, "In Brokenness You Shine," I heard the Lord speak these words into my heart: "Jonathan, this is for you." After that, it seemed as though the crowded auditorium became strangely vacant and Green was singing just to me and to no one else.

The lyrics pierced my soul and ignited the process through which the Lord calmed my fears and restored wholeness to my soul. As I reflected on the words Green sang, I wrote the following in my journal the next night:

> Imagine a glass vase broken into hundreds of pieces scattered about on the floor. Humanly speaking, that is my life right now. My hopes and dreams have all been shattered. The person I thought I was or could become is all gone. Everything in my life is broken; I am broken—reduced to emotions I do not understand and a life I do not want. My hopes, dreams, and aspirations are like the pieces of glass from the vase on the floor, shattered beyond recognition and any hope of restoration....

> But last night Steve Green sang a song about the Lord's beauty shining or showing itself best in our brokenness. How can that be? What can God do with a shattered, despised, and broken vessel? How can he make the scattered pieces shine again?

As I jotted down my thoughts, I sensed a glimmer of confidence as the perspective of eternity began to illuminate the shattered pieces of my life. I ended my journal entry expressing my determination to grab hold of an eternal focus once again:

> The pain and guilt that I feel are intense. I could have made better choices. I could have been stronger. I could have done a thousand things better and nobler. But does it really matter now? Was not God the One who ultimately engineered the shattering of my hopes and my current broken condition?
>
> And if that is true, then I have to believe that God's purpose for me is still alive and well. This is not the path I would have chosen for my life, but then again, God asks us to trust and lean not on our own understanding. He also promises to work everything for the good of those who love him and are called according to His purpose.
>
> So, it comes down to three words: I Still Believe!
>
> **Despite** the shattering of my dreams, I still believe God can work His purposes through me—mine is not to wonder how or why.
>
> **Despite** my brokenness, I still believe in a God of healing and restoration.
>
> **Despite** the ugliness of my current situation, I still believe the Lord's beauty is shining somehow and will shine in the brokenness.

Despite hearing "no" to many of my prayers, I still believe He hears me and has my absolute best interests at heart.

Despite the loss of all my aspirations, I still believe the Lord has wonders in store for me in this life and especially in eternity that will far exceed all my dreams.

Despite the shame, regrets, and wild emotions, I still believe Christ will one day show off His righteousness in me for all to see.

Despite the rejection I feel, I still believe the God of this universe loves me.

Despite the fear I feel, I still believe I am safe and secure in God's arms. He is my rock and strong tower.

I STILL BELIEVE!!

The Lord didn't heal the wounds of my heart immediately following the writing of these words; I had much to absorb in the years after that night. My declaration of hope did, however, set my heart on a path to placing a much higher value on eternal realities. This brought a sorely needed change to the earthbound outlook of my past.

The Rugged Path to Healing

The Lord used two books by John Eldredge to soothe my long-suppressed and ignored wounds. The insights from his book *Desire* brought great relief to the feelings of guilt and shame that had lingered deep inside since I was a teenager and that had grown through two broken marriages. I felt a sense of freedom as I read the book; I wasn't responsible for the abuse that had come my way during the past.

The Lord used another of Eldredge's books, *Wild at Heart,* to identify the wound in my heart that had led to so much dysfunction in my life. Eldredge explained that to experience God's healing, I needed to understand the nature of my deepest injury. How did it happen? What was I afraid of? What exactly was the long-buried fear behind my ongoing panic attacks?

I asked God to reveal the answers to these questions, as Eldredge suggested, and waited to hear from Him. He responded by using the nighttime bouts with my adversary to unveil the worries that had for so long hidden beneath my consciousness.

Rather than suppress my anxieties or fight off the demon-inspired attacks as I had done in the past, I allowed the Lord to use my nightmarish terrors to quiet my soul. Instead of running from my feelings of panic, I stood my ground, waiting for God to give me understanding of what had remained buried for so long.

This pattern reached a climax one night when the Lord used a lengthy encounter with my enemy to reveal the nature of my deepest wound, a deep and long-held inner conviction of being utterly unlovable, unworthy of love, and undesirable to others. This deep lesion in my soul likely began with the intense and brutal bullying I had endured in high school, and it later deepened with the rejection, abuse, and betrayal I experienced in my marriages.

This revelation came with many tears as Jesus took me deep into the cause of my crippling anxieties that had plagued me for so long and led to so many poor and foolish decisions. This became a significant turning point in my battle with PTSD, as my panic attacks diminished significantly in both frequency and intensity after that night.

A Purpose Amid the Pain

In the midst our failures, it's easy think we've forever blown it. That's what I once believed, and Satan was more than happy to reinforce this erroneous assumption. If we let him, our adversary will continue reminding us of our past shortcomings and use them to drive us deeper into panic and despair rather than to the Lord, where we find grace and forgiveness.

The words to the Steve Green song, "In Brokenness You Shine," stress believing the Lord to "bring hope alive" amid brokenness and despair. For me, that meant trusting God's promises of great blessings in eternity despite the great ugliness of my circumstances at the time. It signified putting more weight on the joy ahead for me than on my current experiences, the essence of a life balanced between now and forever, as Paul wrote about in Romans 8:18.

Everything matters to our loving Heavenly Father, even the shattered pieces of our lives strewn about the floor with seemingly no possibility of restoration. He uses all our experiences, even the painful ones in which we suffer much loss, to accomplish His purpose both now as well as in Jesus' future kingdom.

This came to life for me one day after I received an assignment from David C. Cook to write an adult Sunday school lesson from a passage in the book of Proverbs with a focus on the importance of "good words." I remember sitting on my couch one morning thinking and praying about how to approach the subject. The Lord responded to my pleas by speaking this into my heart: "Jonathan, this lesson is right in your wheelhouse." ("Wheelhouse" is a baseball term for a batter receiving a pitch he can hit out of the park, but it's not a word I ever would have thought of on my own.)

With this new insight, I jumped to my feet and raced to my computer. I felt encouraged by the thought that the Lord could use the verbal abuse of my past to add conviction to my writing. Of course, I couldn't incorporate any specifics into the lesson, but I could emphasize the necessity of using our words to build up others up in their walk with the Lord rather than to tear them down.

The Savior's Love

In the lyrics of "In Brokenness You Shine," Green used the phrase "your love surrounds." These words came alive for me several years after his concert.

After work one day, I went for a five-mile run while listening to songs of praise on my iPad Shuffle. Later, I spent time alone with the Lord in prayer. Recent events had caused some nagging worries to resurface. I began my time of praying by submitting my future anew to the Lord and confessing the troublesome anxieties that had crept back into my soul.

A few moments later, I asked the Lord: "If you were seated next to me, what would you say?" I'm not sure what caused me to ask that, but before I even finished my request, I sensed His response: "I love you!" Tears streamed down my face from joy and amazement. Through Jesus' simple words of reassurance, I experienced His love as never before.

The touch of my Savior's love that evening vanquished the remaining impact of PTSD upon my life. With those simple words, the Lord set me free from the burdens, shame, and guilt of my past and brought a wonderful, lasting peace to my heart.

I later experienced my Savior's love in another remarkable way. After many additional years of singleness, the Lord brought a very special woman, Ruth, into my life. In our relationship, I have found a degree of love and acceptance I had long believed were impossible in a marriage. I couldn't have written this book without her loving support, encouragement, and honest feedback.

I might not have considered remarriage had it not been for my pastor at the time. After we spent a two-hour lunch together discussing marriage and my past experiences, he said, "I never want to hear that you've given up on marriage. There's a kind woman out there just for you." I had expected him to tell me that I should never again consider remarriage. His counsel, along with similar advice from two other godly men whose opinions I valued, gave me the courage to contemplate the prospect of marrying again.

I don't understand why the Lord has blessed me in such astounding ways! I certainly don't deserve the grace, forgiveness, and many blessings He continues to send my way. All I know is that Jesus is gracious and compassionate beyond all I could ever have imagined. He forgave my sins and restored my life in ways I had once considered utterly impossible.

This is *my story*, my testimony, of how the Lord's purpose can shine in the darkness of times. He has woven everything, including my many failures and shortcomings, into a mosaic that perfectly fits within the purpose He has had for me from the beginning. I'm thankful for the times of affliction, and I dread the thought of what I might have become apart from the Lord's redirection—albeit painful—of my aspirations and values.

More Than Conquerors

I love the words in Romans 8:35 and 37; they speak to God's unfailing love for us regardless of what comes our way:

> Who shall separate us from the love of Christ? Shall tribulation, or distress, or persecution, or famine, or nakedness, or danger, or sword?... No, in all these things we are more than conquerors through him who loved us.

In Christ, regardless of the storms in our lives or the perilous times in which we live, we *know* that someday we will share in His *triumph* and reign with Him during the Millennium and then forevermore. "We are more than conquerors" because of Jesus and the eternal promises He's now at work bringing to fruition in all the many moments of our lives. Through the afflictions that came my way, I learned that *we are never victims of our circumstances or the behavior of others; rather, we're "conquerors" because of Jesus and His great, unfailing love.*

In the last section of this book, I describe five ways in which we'll someday share in Jesus' victory over sin and death, *our future triumph as redeemed saints.*

Before we explore the wonders of the astounding adventures ahead for us in eternity, we must establish a firm biblical basis for this future hope that makes us "more than conquerors." This is because Satan uses false teaching, along with a widespread lack of biblical knowledge, to attack the three key pillars of our future triumph in Christ: premillennialism, the pre-Tribulation Rapture (i.e., the Lord comes for His Church before the start of the seven-year Tribulation), and the prophetic biblical texts that support these truths.

As we examine the biblical foundation of our hope, it will become apparent why these truths are so vital to a two-world perspective that *seizes* future kingdom realities, brings our anticipation of future glory into the present, and calms anxious hearts.

Section Two

The Foundation of Living with An Eternal Perspective

Premillennialism provides the key foundation for placing our "blessed hope" (Titus 2:11–14) before the start of the seven-year Tribulation. If one dismisses what the Bible says about the literalness of the Tribulation and Jesus' thousand-year reign over the nations as do amillennialists, it doesn't matter what one believes about the placement of the Rapture in regard to the Tribulation.

If the judgments of the Tribulation are not future and real events, then we have nothing to miss with a pre-Tribulation Rapture. It means little to believe in a post-Tribulation Rapture if one dismisses all judgments of Tribulation as allegory or history from the first century. *That's why it's essential to first establish a firm foundation in premillennialism.*

For my purposes in this book, premillennial beliefs consist of the following:

- The future appearing of Jesus to take His Church back to heaven (John 14:2–3). Most premillennialists place the Rapture before

the Tribulation, but others put it in the middle or at the end of this coming time of judgment.
- A literal seven-year Tribulation as described in Revelation chapters 6–18.
- Jesus' glorious return to the earth at the end of the Tribulation, but before His thousand-year reign over the nations of the world (Revelation chapters 19–20).
- The restoration of a glorious kingdom for a repentant Israel (Zechariah 12–14).

My overriding passion is for readers to understand the importance of this essential foundation for maintaining an eternal perspective during the perilous times in which we live. Our adversary, the devil, uses false teachings to deny us the encouragement we need to face uncertain days. He does all he can to prevent us from seeing beyond the darkness of this world to the joyous inheritance that awaits us in eternity.

Premillennialism, as described in the earlier bullet points, is essential for a gospel-driven, eternal perspective of life. It alone supports the biblical teaching of our *imminent* anticipation of Jesus' appearing (Philippians 3:20–21) and our thrilling reign with Him during the Millennium (Revelation 5:9–10). Apart from these foundations, one's hope consists of a dull and sign-less return of Jesus to wrap up things for the current age.

To establish a scriptural basis for premillennialism, I will emphasize the Lord's promises to the nation of Israel. All amillennial viewpoints—and by that I refer to all those that deny a literal thousand-year reign of Christ over the nations of the world—interpret biblical prophecies regarding the coming restoration of Israel as symbolic, and most apply these promises to the Church.

Please prayerfully consider the passages of Scripture cited in these chapters and the specifics of our hope that we can glean from the *words* in these texts. See if the Lord speaks to you in same way that He does to me. Examine what each passage says without overlaying its meaning with preconceived paradigms garnered from human wisdom. Ask yourself if these supporting arguments in favor of premillennialism fit with what the *words* of the Bible say, or not.

Does God's Word foretell a magnificent reestablishment of a kingdom for Israel? I absolutely believe it does, and in the chapters that follow I present a biblical case for such a conclusion.

4

God's Faithfulness to Israel Secures Our Hope

> The question of the Millennial kingdom is therefore not only a question of final history, but touches at the same time the very heart of the gospel (freedom from law, universality of the gospel, gift by grace). To deny it makes either God a liar in relation to His prophesies or Paul a false witness to us. Rom[ans] 9–11 is no mere justifying of God, but a justification of Paul's doctrine of justification.
>
> –Erich Sauer, *The Triumph of the Crucified*[10]

"Israel's future guarantees our salvation."[11]

At first glance, the above statement might seem absurd. How can Israel's future have anything to do with our redemption as New Testament saints? Why would God's relationship with Israel matter to our eternal destiny?

Consider this: If God can break His covenants with such Old Testament champions of the faith as Abraham, Isaac, Jacob, and David, what does that say about His promises regarding our salvation? If God can renege on His unconditional promises to Israel, ones He repeated many times throughout the writings of the prophets and in the Psalms, what does that say about our security?

Do you see why God's unconditional covenants with Israel matter? Their continued validity is not some meaningless squabble reserved for stuffy theologians in drab seminary classrooms. This debate has far-reaching implications for each of us; it speaks to our security as the redeemed of the Lord. It greatly matters when we put our heads on the pillow at night wondering what the next day might bring our way.

In words one cannot mistake, Paul says in Romans 11:1–2:

> I ask, then, has God rejected his people? By no means! For I myself am an Israelite, a descendant of Abraham, a member of the tribe of Benjamin. God has not rejected his people whom he foreknew.

The apostle makes it clear that he is talking about the physical Israel as he asserts in no uncertain terms that God has not rejected His people. He will keep His promises to Israel!

The apostle later adds, "For the gifts and the calling of God are irrevocable" (Romans 11:29). The Lord will never renege on His covenants with Israel or on His promises to us. His grace will never fail us; our salvation is irreversible.

Now it's time to get down to the nitty-gritty of why I believe God will someday restore a glorious kingdom to Israel. Please stay with me as I build a case from God's Word.

It Begins with a Question

I like to begin the defense of Israel's continuing place in God's prophetic program with the question the disciples asked Jesus moments before He ascended into heaven: "Lord, will you at this time restore the kingdom to Israel?" (Acts 1:6). Earlier, this hope had led to arguments among the disciples as to which of them would have the top spots in Jesus' kingdom

(Mark 10:35–40). Although such quarrelling seems to have ended after Christ's crucifixion and resurrection, the disciples' dream of a reestablished kingdom for Israel did not.

Pay careful attention to the Savior's response to the disciples: "It is not for you to know times or seasons that the Father has fixed by his own authority" (Acts 1:7). Jesus didn't contradict, ridicule, or refute the premise of their question. Instead, He told them they could not know the *timing* of when He would establish Israel as a magnificent kingdom, as that was something the Father had "fixed by his own authority."

This interaction is crucial to understanding Israel's future. First, after listening to Jesus teach about prophecy and the kingdom after His resurrection (Acts 1:3), the disciples remained convinced that He would return Israel to a place of greatness in the future. The explanations Jesus gave during this time did not dash their hope regarding a future kingdom for the descendants of Jacob.

Second, Jesus said nothing to quell the anticipation of His disciples in response to their inquiry; He told them that their timing was off and diverted their attention to the task at hand: the proclamation of the gospel to a lost world (Acts 1:8). He did not diminish their hopes.

Why Would They Ask Such a Question?

The confidence of the disciples regarding such a future for Israel raises questions in my mind. After watching the Jewish rulers reject Christ and demand His crucifixion, what made the disciples think the Lord would immediately restore the kingdom to them? Why did they assume that Jesus would initiate a spectacular renewal for the very same people whose rejection had led to His being mocked, to His vicious scourging, and to His bloody crucifixion?

Many theologians throughout history have used the Jewish rejection of Jesus to justify their belief that God has forever rejected Israel and replaced it with the Church. But not the disciples, the very ones who watched their fellow Israelites reject and condemn their beloved Master. They still anticipated a future restoration of the kingdom.

What made them so sure?

After His resurrection, Jesus expounded on how He fulfilled prophecy. Beginning with the two on the road to Emmaus and later with the disciples in the upper room, Jesus explained that He fulfilled *all* the Old Testament Scriptures (Luke 24:25–27, 44–47). In addition to His careful instruction in Old Testament prophecy, Luke 24:45 tells us that the Lord "opened" the minds of the disciples "to understand the Scriptures." Their question sprang from a wealth of great teaching on the matter and a comprehension supernaturally aided by Jesus.

Those who say the disciples' query in Acts 1:6 represents a continuation of their bumbling foolishness overlook four other critical factors.

First, they ignore the teaching Jesus gave the disciples after His resurrection (Acts 1:3). What does it say about Christ's training of His future apostles if they remained confused on such an important and essential matter as God's kingdom promises to Israel, especially after He had talked extensively to them about this subject after His resurrection?

Second, they fail to acknowledge that Jesus didn't regard the question as foolish or negate its premise! *The Lord said nothing to challenge their basic assumption; He only disagreed with the timing.*

If the disciples had woefully missed the point of Jesus' teaching about His kingdom and what that meant for the future of Israel, the Lord would surely have answered them in a way similar to how He responded to Philip in the upper room when he asked to see the Father. Jesus didn't hesitate to correct his error: "Have I been with you so long and you still do not know me, Philip?" (John 14:9).

Would Jesus have let such a critical misreading of kingdom promises remain in the minds of His disciples moments before His ascension? I believe He would have corrected them if indeed they had misunderstood His teaching regarding the future of Israel.

Third, those who mock the disciples' question in Acts 1:6 fail to note the significance that the Lord promised to "restore the fortunes" of Israel at least ten times throughout the Psalms and the books of the prophets (see Psalm 14:7; Jeremiah 30:18; 31:23; 33:11; Ezekiel 39:25; Hosea 6:11; Joel 3:1; Amos 9:14). The apostles had a solid scriptural basis for their question. Their question repeated verbatim the many texts they had read in Scripture.

Fourth, those who discredit the disciples' question overlook Jesus' words in Matthew 19:28:

> Truly, I say to you, in the new world, when the Son of Man will sit on his glorious throne, you who have followed me will also sit on twelve thrones, judging the twelve tribes of Israel.

The Lord repeated this, with slightly different wording, in Luke 22:28–30.

The disciples' question in Acts 1:6 confirms that they took the Lord's words in Matthew 19:28 to constitute a real, physical kingdom for Israel. It also signifies that Jesus did not negate this understanding in His discussions of Israel's future kingdom after His resurrection. Jesus assured them of a future place in ruling over Israel, and He let their assumption of just such a kingdom stand moments before He ascended to heaven. Why would He do that if it wasn't true?

If the events surrounding the crucifixion had voided Jesus' pledge to His followers in Matthew 19:28, or if they had misunderstood the nature of the coming kingdom, Jesus had ample opportunity to correct the disciples' flawed assumptions after His resurrection. Instead, He affirmed the belief of His followers regarding a future restored kingdom for Israel with His answer in Acts 1:7 that only voided their understanding of the timing, not their key premise.

As we will see in the following sections, the Old Testament prophets validate the disciples' confidence regarding God's future renewal of a kingdom for Israel.

Jeremiah's Unmistakable Affirmation of Israel's Future Restoration

Jeremiah prophesied that God would restore Israel and Judah together as one nation. Notice the similarity of the wording in Jeremiah 30:1–3 to that of the disciples' question in Acts 1:6:

> The word that came to Jeremiah from the LORD: "Thus says the LORD, the God of Israel: Write in a book all the words that I have spoken to you. For behold, days are coming, declares the LORD, when I will **restore the fortunes** of my people, Israel and Judah, says the LORD, and I will bring them back to the land that I gave to their fathers, and they shall take possession of it." (Emphasis added)

This prophecy cannot apply to Judah's return from captivity in Babylon, because Jeremiah's promised restoration includes both "Israel and Judah." Such a reestablished and combined kingdom hasn't existed since the early days of King Rehoboam, the son of Solomon. The promise in the above prophecy from Jeremiah remains unfulfilled.

Jeremiah 30:9 adds this to the promise regarding Israel's future:

> But they shall serve the LORD their God and David their king, whom I will raise up for them.

Since the days of Jeremiah, no descendant of David has ever ruled over Israel. Jesus alone possesses the proper lineage to sit on the nation's throne (see Isaiah 9:6–7). Jeremiah 31:35–36 provides an unshakeable affirmation regarding the continuation of Israel as a nation:

> Thus says the LORD, who gives the sun for light by day and the fixed order of the moon and the stars for light by night, who

> stirs up the sea so that its waves roar—the LORD of hosts is his name: "If this fixed order departs from before me, declares the Lord then shall the offspring of Israel cease from being a nation before me forever."

In words that appear irrefutable, the Lord tells us through the prophet Jeremiah that Israel will not cease to be a nation as long as the fixed order of day and night continues. If the sun comes up tomorrow, it signifies that Israel persists as a nation before the Lord. If we see the moon or the stars in the nighttime sky, Israel endures as God's chosen people. Jeremiah 31:35–36 leaves no doubt regarding God's intention to bless and restore the nation of Israel at a still future time.

God will fulfill His promises to His people. He remains faithful forever to His covenants, which remain in effect to this day.

God Has Not Rejected Israel

Jeremiah didn't record God's promises about Israel during a time of national faithfulness; quite the contrary. He did so in the midst of warning the people of Judah about dire consequences that would befall them unless they repented of their wickedness (Jeremiah 21:3–10). During the prophet's lifetime, Nebuchadnezzar and the Babylonians ransacked Jerusalem, destroyed the Temple, and took a great many people from Judah into captivity in Babylon.

The prophet's repeated warnings of judgment caused many in Jerusalem to mistakenly conclude that Israel had no future; like many today, they believed God had forever rejected them. Notice the Lord's response in Jeremiah 33:26, which applies today as well:

> The word of the Lord came to Jeremiah: "Have you not observed that these people are saying, 'The LORD has rejected the two

> clans that he chose?' Thus they have despised my people so that they are no longer a nation in their sight. Thus says the LORD: If I have not established my covenant with day and night and the fixed order of heaven and earth, then I will reject the offspring of Jacob and David my servant and will not choose one of his offspring to rule over the offspring of Abraham, Isaac, and Jacob. For I will **restore their fortunes** and will have mercy on them." (Emphasis added)

In this text, Jeremiah forcibly negates any notion of God rejecting Israel by repeating his earlier declaration that God's forever choice of the Israelites as His people is just as certain as His "covenant with day and night and the fixed order of heaven and earth."

Jeremiah's prophecies, as do those of other Old Testament prophets, explain the confidence of the disciples regarding the Lord's intention to "restore the kingdom to Israel."

Other Prophets Repeat God's Promise to Restore Israel

Isaiah, who lived a hundred years before the time of Jeremiah, proclaimed a similar message to Judah. He warned the people of impending judgment because of their rebellion and idolatry, and, like Jeremiah, Isaiah often foretold a magnificent future of Israel with a descendant of David as its king.

Jesus will fulfill the mention of Him as the "root of Jesse" in Isaiah 11:10:

> In that day the root of Jesse, who shall stand as a signal for the peoples—of him shall the nations inquire, and his resting place shall be glorious.

These words not only gave hope to the faithful in Jerusalem at the time, but also assured them that God's judgment of their current sins did not signify the end of Israel:

> The nations shall see your righteousness, and all the kings your glory.... You shall be a crown of beauty in the hand of the Lord, and a royal diadem in the hand of your God. (Isaiah 62:2–3)

In Isaiah 54:10, the Lord gave His people this reassurance:

> "For the mountains may depart and the hills be removed, but my steadfast love shall not depart from you, and my covenant of peace shall not be removed," says the LORD, who has compassion on you.

These words sound similar to those recorded in the book of Jeremiah.

Zephaniah also spoke of a future foregathering of Israel as a kingdom with these words:

> At that time I will bring you in, at the time when I gather you together; for I will make you renowned and praised among all the peoples of the earth, when I **restore your fortunes** before your eyes, says the Lord. (Zephaniah 3:20, emphasis added)

Has this ever happened? No, this prophecy awaits fulfillment.

Despite the dire warnings of judgment for Judah throughout his book, the prophet Joel concludes with strong reassurances for Jerusalem:

> So you shall know that I am the LORD your God, who dwells in Zion, my holy mountain. And Jerusalem shall be holy and strangers shall never again pass through it.... But Judah shall be inhabited forever, and Jerusalem to all generations. (Joel 3:17, 20)

Joel leaves no room for doubt; the Lord will someday return Jerusalem to a place of prominence in the world such as the city has never before experienced in history.

In Amos 9:14–15, the prophet says this on behalf of the Lord:

> I will **restore the fortunes** of my people Israel.... I will plant them on their land, and they shall never again be uprooted out of the land that I have given them. (Amos 9:15, emphasis added)

This could not be any clearer: The Lord will *permanently* bring the people of Israel back to their land, something He hasn't yet done but will do in the future. What we see today is just the beginning of God's purposes for regathering His people.

In Zechariah 8:4–5, the Lord describes a scene of remarkable peace and safety in Jerusalem as a result of His presence in the city:

> Thus says the LORD of hosts: Old men and old women shall again sit in the streets of Jerusalem, each with staff in hand because of great age. And the streets of the city shall be full of boys and girls playing in its streets.

When will such a time of security and serenity on the streets of Jerusalem happen? The Lord gives us the answer a couple of verses later:

> Behold, I will save my people from the east country and from the west country, and I will bring them to dwell in the midst of Jerusalem. And they shall be my people, and I will be their God, in faithfulness and in righteousness. (Zechariah 8:7–8).

The scene on the streets of Jerusalem envisioned by the prophet takes place when the Lord brings His people back to the land and dwells with them. This is the Millennium, the thousand-year reign of Jesus over the nations of the world, about which John wrote in Revelation 20:1–10. Zechariah 14 describes Jesus' universal rule from the city of Jerusalem.

Did the disciples have a solid scriptural basis for their question in Acts 1:6? Absolutely! They not only knew the many assurances of the ancient prophets, but they had also spent weeks listening to Jesus teach them about His kingdom and how He fulfilled prophecy.

Why is this so important to believers living in the twenty-first century?

Because God will surely restore a future kingdom for Israel, we can absolutely count on His faithfulness toward us. He will keep *all* the promises He has made to us.

Because God remains faithful to His covenants with the likes of Abraham, Isaac, Jacob, and David, we rest assured that He will not fail to bring all of His redeemed (that's us) safely to the paradise that awaits us.

5

Israel's Future Restoration Vindicates God's Holiness

The heart that is in line with the purposes of God will pray fervently that the hour may not be far off when repentant Israel will look upon their pierced Messiah and own Him as their Shepherd, their Lord, their King, and their Saviour.

~Charles L. Feinberg, *God Remembers*[12]

The certainty of the Lord fulfilling His oft-repeated promise to restore the fortunes of Israel, as discussed in the previous chapter, is a necessary component of God's righteous character. *Israel's future restoration vindicates His holiness.*

You probably think I'm a bit out of my mind for making such a statement. How can I say that Israel's still-future restoration preserves God's integrity? Doesn't that seem extreme, even for an avid old premillennialist such as myself?

I begin the defense of my sanity with what the Lord said in Ezekiel 36:22–24:

> Therefore say to the house of Israel, Thus says the Lord God: It is not for your sake, O house of Israel, that I am about to act, but for the sake of my holy name, which you have profaned among the nations to which you came. And I will vindicate the holiness of my great name, which has been profaned among the nations, and which you have profaned among them. And the nations will know that I am the LORD, declares the Lord God, when through you I vindicate my holiness before their eyes. I will take you from the nations and gather you from all the countries and bring you into your own land.

God will at some point intervene in history on behalf of Israel, and when He does, it will not happen based on any inherent goodness on the part of His chosen people. He will, rather, act in order to "vindicate" His righteous character.

You see, there's much more at stake than just the reestablishment of a flourishing kingdom for Israel. God's keeping of His covenants with and pledges to Israel sets Him apart from all other recipients of worship. It proves His power to remain worthy of our trust throughout history and demonstrates His unshakeable determination to do so. There's no one else like Him; He's the almighty and sovereign God over all. He forever remains true to His Word, and that preserves the veracity of His righteousness.

For us, this signifies that when Jesus assures us of eternal life, such as He did in John 10:27–30, we can know with absolute certainty that He will keep His word.

Because so many in the church today deny that God will someday restore Israel, let's look more in depth at what this passage reveals, and later we'll see what Zechariah chapters 12–14 disclose about the future repentance.

Promises That Will Vindicate God's Holy Character

How do we know the Ezekiel 36:22–38 restoration of Israel lies in the future? We know this because God hasn't yet fulfilled many of the events and circumstances detailed in the passage.

Verse 27 says:

> And I will put my Spirit within you, and cause you to walk in my statutes and be careful to obey my rules.

We know from John 16:7–11 that the Holy Spirit could only come in such a personal way *after* the death, resurrection, and ascension of Jesus. God could not have fulfilled Ezekiel's prophecy before the time of Christ or even while He was walking on the earth, because it points to a time when the Lord will put His Spirit in the hearts of the Jewish people. This could only happen after Jesus' ascension into heaven; the fulfillment of these verses thus awaits a future time.

Since the time of Christ, we haven't seen any of the words of this passage come to full fruition. Although we see glimpses of the blessings spoken of in Ezekiel 36:22–38, the Lord hasn't yet given the Jewish people all the benefits promised, which include:

- Israelites from the countries of the world will gather into their land (v. 24).
- The Israelites' sins will be cleansed (vv. 25, 26).
- God will place His Spirit, along with a new heart, within them (v. 26).
- Israel will dwell in the land that God gave to the patriarchs (v. 28).
- The land once desolate will become like the Garden of Eden and produce an abundant harvest (vv. 28–35).

If the words of the prophet Ezekiel matter, and they do, then we understand that God has not yet given His people all the blessings that He promised in these verses.

The reuniting of Israel as a nation will vindicate the Lord's righteous character as a promise-keeping God; Israel will receive the blessings listed above because the Lord is a holy and covenant-keeping God. If He were to default on His solemn Word, it would stain His holy character, and that is impossible.

The Lord will keep His promises to Israel in spite of, not because of, that nation's behavior.

Israel Will Repent at Jesus' Return to the Earth

In Ezekiel 36:25–26, the Lord refers to a time when He will cleanse His people from their sins, give them a new heart, and fill them with His Holy Spirit (something that can only happen after the Day of Pentecost).

Zechariah 12:10–13:1 tells us when this will happen:

> And I will pour out on the house of David and the inhabitants of Jerusalem a spirit of grace and pleas for mercy, so that, when they look on me, on him whom they have pierced, they shall mourn for him, as one mourns for an only child, and weep bitterly over him, as one weeps over a firstborn. (v. 10)

This recognition of their Messiah, the one "they have pierced," will open the door to God pouring out His Spirit upon the Jewish people. The prophet Joel connects this event with the Second Coming (Joel 2:28–32) as does the Apostle John in Revelation 1:7.

Zechariah goes to considerable lengths to identify the subjects of this later repentance as Israelites. Who else could he describe as looking "on him whom they have pierced?" As further confirmation that this great change of heart refers solely to the descendants of Jacob, the remaining verses of chapter 12 and the first verse of chapter 13 leave no room for doubt; this cannot refer to the Church or to anyone else but people of Israel.

Zechariah Repeats God's Promise of a Kingdom

Zechariah's prophecy of Israel's repentance becomes all the more significant when we consider what he wrote a couple of chapters later:

> And the Lord will be king over all the earth. On that day the Lord will be one and his name one. (Zechariah 14:9)

The remainder of the chapter describes the battle in which Jesus takes control of the nations of the world as well as the extent of His worldwide kingdom. The Lord, through His prophet, revealed that Jesus would someday reign in Jerusalem and that the extent of His rule will reach to the ends of the earth (see also Zechariah 14:16–21).

Why is this so important?

Please notice that God's foreknowledge of how the Jewish people would treat their Messiah, His Son, didn't stop Him from predicting that the Lord would rule over a kingdom while based in Jerusalem (Zechariah 14:8–11). *The Lord promised Israel a future glorious kingdom with the full awareness that His people would someday crucify His Son.*

The Jewish rejection of Christ didn't surprise God; He knew all about this long before He made His covenants with Israel and forever promised the land to them (Psalm 105:8–11). How could the Lord possibly break a promise based on behavior He knew all about when He made it? Isn't such deception contrary to His character as a righteous God who cannot lie (Titus 1:2)?

The words of Ezekiel 36:22 provide the key:

> Therefore say to the house of Israel, Thus says the Lord God: It is not for your sake, O house of Israel, that I am about to act, but for the sake of my holy name, which you have profaned among the nations to which you came.

God will someday act on behalf of Israel because His character keeps Him from voiding the many assurances He gave to His people of a future renewal of a kingdom for them.

Why Does This Matter?

Consider this. If God can renege on assurances based on actions that He knew all about when He made those promises, doesn't it cast an ominous shadow over our expectations for eternal life? Such action implies that God not only is capable of failing to carry out His pledges, but is willing to do so based on behavior He knew all about when He promised us eternal life.

Did God know about all our sins (past, present, and future) when He pronounced us righteous at the time of our salvation (our justification)? Absolutely! Just as with the people of Israel, we never surprise the Lord by anything we do or say, as bad as it might seem at the time. It's impossible to catch Him unaware by anything awful we do; it cannot happen.

The Lord knew about all our future sins when He pronounced us forever righteous based on Jesus' sacrifice on our behalf. We can't nullify our justification with our behavior, which is the basis of Paul's comforting words in Roman 8:31–39. We remain absolutely secure in Christ in spite of our inability to live perfect lives or remain connected to Him at all times.

Our security as New Testament saints rests in a promise-keeping God who cannot nullify His Word to us just as He cannot break His promises to Israel. Such remarkable love invigorates us all the more to serve our wonderful Savior.

6

God Keeps His Covenants

> The Abrahamic covenant.... Since it was unconditional and eternal, and has never yet been fulfilled, it must await a future fulfillment; Israel must be preserved as a nation, must inherit her land, and be blessed with spiritual blessings to make this inheritance possible.
>
> -J. Dwight Pentecost, *Things to Come*[13]

What I regard as a variation of amillennialism, "covenant premillennialism" states that Jesus fulfilled all God's covenants with Israel at His First Coming. While proponents of this theology disagree with amillennialists on many details, they agree in their denial of a literal thousand-year reign of Jesus on the throne of David as the Lord promised through the prophet Isaiah and later through the angel Gabriel (Isaiah 9:6–7; Luke 1:32–33). Despite their claim to be premillennial, I consider them amillennialists because they deny the validity of a literal thousand-year reign of Jesus by assigning an allegorical interpretation to Revelation 20:1–10.

Amillennialists combine the biblical promises of the Millennium with the Church Age; covenant premillennialists merge them with the eternal state. Both groups *retrofit* prophetic texts concerning Israel's future based on a preconceived ideology. They thus negate the original intention of the prophets and fail to recognize how God is beginning to fulfill His eternal promises, which began with the miraculous rebirth of Israel.

The Miracle of Israel's Existence

Those who believe that God's covenants with Israel no longer remain in effect overlook the miracle of how Israel became a nation and has since survived the fierce opposition of the Arab world. Apart from God's supernatural intervention, how can we possibly explain the reappearance of a nation with its original language after a two-thousand-year absence? *Israel's current existence is a supernatural occurrence of immense proportions.*

The prophet Isaiah asked long ago, "Shall a land be born in one day? Shall a nation be brought forth in one moment?" (Isaiah 66:8). The answer is, "Oh, yes!" On May 14, 1948, God fulfilled this impossible-sounding prophecy: Israel became a nation in a day. It's impossible to overstate the significance of this or dismiss it as a mere coincidence. The rebirth of the nation was a spectacular fulfillment of prophecy such as only God could do.

In Ezekiel 36:35, the Lord promised that the once-desolate land of Israel would someday be like the Garden of Eden. We see a similar assurance in Isaiah 27:6:

> In days to come Jacob shall take root, Israel shall blossom and put forth shoots and fill the world with fruit.

Today, Israel is one of the top exporters of produce. Despite the barren and desolate condition of the land in 1948, that nation now exports $1 billion of fruit each year. How is that even remotely possible apart from the Lord's intervention during the past several years?

As the Six Day War of 1967 approached, Israel had an army of seventy-five thousand compared with that of five hundred thousand soldiers amassed against them. Israel's enemies had five thousand tanks compared to their one thousand. The Arab countries had nine hundred military aircraft compared to 175 for Israel. Yet despite Israel's overwhelming disadvantage, the nation not only decisively defeated its enemies, but did so in just six days! Numerous reports from soldiers involved in this war confirm that God literally fought for Israel.

This victory ranks right alongside Gideon's defeat of the Midianites recorded in Judges 7, as well as many other spectacular military wins when God fought for Israel. Humanly speaking, Israel's enemies should have ended its existence as a nation in 1967, but the Lord intervened in a miraculous way that was quite similar to how He fought for the nation in the Old Testament.

Why did the Lord save Israel from annihilation in 1967? Because He still intends to keep His covenants with that nation and restore its kingdom, just as He promised in the Old Testament.

In Luke 12:54–56, Jesus scolded the crowds listening to Him teach for their lack of perception regarding the day in which they lived. Although they readily recognized the signs of approaching weather, they missed all prophetic indications of the Messiah's presence in their midst. I believe Jesus would similarly reprimand those today who do not recognize the prophetic significance of Israel's restoration as a nation as well as the many other signals that indicate we live in the last days of human history as we know it.

The Bible said these things would happen, and now we see them taking place. We surely live in the last days of human history as we know it.

The Everlasting Covenant of the Land

The miracle of Israel existing as a nation serves as a reminder of God's intention to keep His covenant with the patriarchs regarding the land.

Genesis 15:7–21 records the Lord making this covenant with Abram (later called Abraham). The text says God, not Abram, passed through the carcasses of the dead animals, with half on each side while the patriarch remained in a deep sleep.

Typically, both parties to such an agreement would walk between the halves of the remains, obligating each one to the terms of the covenant. However, in this case, God alone passed through them while Abram slept. By doing so, He made His promise of the land completely dependent upon Himself. He gave the sleeping patriarch and His descendants the land of Canaan with no strings attached. The fulfillment of the land promise depends 100 percent on the Lord.

In 1 Chronicles 16:14–18, we read that David verified the everlasting nature of God's promise of the land to Abraham, Isaac, and the descendants of Jacob:

> He is the LORD our God; his judgments are in all the earth. Remember his covenant forever, the word that he commanded, for a thousand generations, the covenant that he made with Abraham. His sworn promise to Isaac, which he confirmed to Jacob as a statute to Israel as an everlasting covenant, saying, "To you I will give the land of Canaan as your portion for an inheritance."

God couldn't have made it any clearer than He did. *His covenant of the land with Israel is permanent.* Why would He say it's "an everlasting covenant" if He didn't intend for it to be one? If the Lord says a covenant is "everlasting," then it will never come to an end.

God's covenant of the land remains firmly in place. The promise didn't reach fulfillment during Jesus' first appearance on the earth, nor can we apply it to the Church. *This remains unfulfilled in its entirety, but the day is coming when Israel will enjoy all the land promised in Genesis 15:18–21.*

Some might argue that Israel's long absence from the land proves that this covenant is no longer in effect. However, when God made the promise to Abraham's descendants through Isaac and Jacob, He didn't say the Israelites would continuously enjoy its benefits. As evidence of this, the Lord spoke of a four-hundred-year gap when Abraham's descendants wouldn't be in the land after the time that He made this covenant (Genesis 15:13).

In Deuteronomy chapters 27–28, Moses revealed the blessings Israel would enjoy in the land as the result of their obedience, then he warned of the dire consequences of turning away from the Lord, such as exile among the nations of the world. God conditioned Israel's *enjoyment* of the Promised Land on the nation's obedience, but Israel's *inheritance* of it was unconditional.[14] *The land forever belongs to the children of Israel based on God's unconditional covenant, but the nation's enjoyment of it depends on their obedience, as specified by Moses.*

Israel's long absence from the land doesn't nullify God's "everlasting covenant"; we haven't yet reached the end of "everlasting." The land still belongs to the descendants of Jacob!

The New Covenant

Through the prophets Jeremiah and Ezekiel, God promised that He would make a new covenant with Israel. In Jeremiah 31:31–32, the Lord said:

> Behold, the days are coming, declares the LORD, when I will make a new covenant with the house of Israel and the house of Judah, not like the covenant that I made with their fathers on the day when I took them by the hand to bring them out of the land of Egypt, my covenant that they broke, though I was their husband, declares the Lord.

Ezekiel 36:24–28 describes this new covenant as a time when God will purify His people, give them a new heart, and pour out His Spirit within them; once again, the Israelites will dwell in the land (Ezekiel 36:33–38). The new covenant doesn't nullify God's prior promise of the land to the Israelites; it comes alongside it.

Both premillennialists and amillennialists believe the promises of this new covenant apply in some way to the Church.[15] The writer of Hebrews quotes the Jeremiah passage and assigns its benefits to New Testament believers (Hebrews 8:8–13). On the night before His crucifixion, Jesus took the cup and said, "This cup is the new covenant in my blood" (1 Corinthians 11:25). Although we as saints enjoy some of the blessings and provisions of the new covenant, it doesn't signify that God has rejected Israel and replaced it with the Church.

Both Jeremiah and Ezekiel prophesy about a restoration for Israel in the same context in which they reveal God's promise of a new covenant. That is key to our understanding. Again, the Lord's inclusion of New Testament believers in the new covenant doesn't invalidate His covenants with Israel or His promises to restore a kingdom to Israel.

Just as the provisions of God's covenant with Abraham led to salvation for all people through the coming of the Savior, so do the blessings of the new covenant apply to both Gentiles and Jews, to both the Church and Israel, at a future time. In other words, the new covenant is an "amplification" of the saving provisions of the original covenant with Abraham.[16]

Israel's Future Assures Us of God's Unfailing Faithfulness

As we saw in the previous chapter, God keeping His covenants with Israel was never contingent upon the obedience of the Israelites, nor will it ever be. In particular, the Lord made His covenant of the land totally dependent upon His faithfulness rather than on the good behavior of Jacob's descendants.

God's faithfulness to the covenants He made with Israel assures us that He will keep all His promises to those of us in Christ. Someday, we will possess glorified and immortal bodies, reign with Jesus in His kingdom, and forever enjoy a restored earth and spectacular city, the New Jerusalem. In the same way that God's covenant with Israel guarantees its future as a nation, the new covenant assures us of a triumphant future in Christ.

God's unflinching faithfulness to Israel gives us a picture of our security in Jesus. Just as He won't fail to keep His promises to Israel, He won't fail to bring all those in Christ safely home to heaven.

The words of Isaiah 54:10 sum up the Lord's resolve to bless His chosen people in the future:

> "For the mountains may depart and the hills be removed, but my steadfast love shall not depart from you, and my covenant of peace shall not be removed," says the Lord, who has compassion on you.

In John 10:27–28, we see Jesus' resolve toward those who come to Him:

> My sheep hear my voice, and I know them, and they follow me. I give them eternal life, and they will never perish, and no one will snatch them out of my hand.

Those in Christ "will never perish"; that's Jesus' loving and unfailing promise.

7

Jesus Will Rule over the Nations of This World

> The evidence is overwhelming that the Old Testament prophets understood that God intended to establish a literal kingdom on earth under the rule of the Messiah.... The angel Gabriel came to Mary and prophesied that Jesus will rule the kingdom from "the throne of his father David."
>
> -Grant R. Jeffrey, *Triumphant Return*[17]

Royalty intrigues us, doesn't it? Consider the popularity of the Netflix series called *The Crown*, which recalls many historical events from the reign of Queen Elizabeth II. Many people also watched a series on PBS, *Victoria*, that depicts the lives of Queen Victoria and Prince Albert. Its popularity turned this short miniseries to a multi-season run.

The success of these shows, along with the popularity of numerous movies with similar themes, points to our fascination with kings and queens. Portrayals of great kingdoms, such as King Arthur's Camelot, that have powerful and benevolent monarchs intrigue us beyond what we might expect.

Ecclesiastes 3:11 says God "has put eternity into [our] hearts." Could the Lord be the source of our fascination with kings, queens, and kingdoms? Is there something deep inside us that speaks to the reality of our coming King, to the reign of Jesus over all the earth? Is the promised Millennium the return to Camelot we crave? I believe it is!

Sir Isaac Newton spent thousands of hours studying the books of Daniel and Revelation during the latter years of his life. As the result of his intense study, the physicist and scientist predicted that Israel would someday become a nation again. (He said this well over two hundred years before it happened.) Furthermore, he believed in a literal Tribulation, in the desecration of a future Jewish Temple by the Antichrist, and in Jesus' return with us to set up His millennial kingdom on earth.

In building a biblical case for a literal kingdom in Israel's future, I will start at the same place Newton did—with the book of Daniel.

Daniel's Interpretation of Nebuchadnezzar's Dream

Daniel 2 records the story of Nebuchadnezzar's prophetic dream. The ancient Babylonian king recognized its significance, but didn't know how to interpret it. To ensure the validity of the interpretation he might receive from his magicians and sorcerers, the king demanded that they reveal the content of the dream as well as its meaning. Failure to do so would result in the violent death of all his magicians and advisors and in the destruction of their homes.

The conditions set by the king were impossible apart from God's intervention. Hearing of the dire consequences of failing to interpret the dream, Daniel requested more time so he and his three friends could pray. The Lord responded by revealing both the dream and its interpretation to Daniel (see Daniel 2:1–20), which he later conveyed to the king.

In his dream, Nebuchadnezzar saw a huge image of a man made of different types of metal in the various sections of its body. Daniel told the king that the head of gold symbolized his kingdom, the mighty

Babylonian empire. The chest and arms of silver, he said, signified the rule of the Medes and Persians—the power that later defeated ancient Babylon and ruled the world after the demise of the Chaldeans.

The bronze midsection and thighs signified the future Greek empire that would overspread the known world under Alexander the Great. Lastly, the legs of iron and feet of mixed iron and clay denoted a final world kingdom that referred to the Roman Empire, with the ten toes symbolizing a still-future adaptation of the worldwide Roman Empire (Daniel 2:31–43).

In the final scene of the dream, a large stone struck and shattered the great image. Daniel identified the rock as God's kingdom:

> And in the days of those kings the God of heaven will set up a kingdom that shall never be destroyed, nor shall the kingdom be left to another people. It shall break in pieces all these kingdoms and bring them to an end, and it shall stand forever. (Daniel 2:44).

During the times of the ten kings, representing the final form of the Roman Empire, the arrival of the Lord's kingdom will destroy all the governmental systems of this world and expand until it fills all the earth.

The later part of Nebuchadnezzar's dream awaits a fulfillment. The rock that brings down the image by striking and destroying the ten toes represents the crushing of all the realms of this world that will occur at Jesus' return to earth. This didn't happen during His First Coming. The Lord didn't suddenly destroy Rome or any other nation then, nor did the Holy Spirit do so at Pentecost.

The "great mountain" (Daniel 2: 35) that fills the earth is Jesus' millennial reign, which He will establish after He destroys the armies of the world at His Second Coming.

A literal understanding of Daniel 2 leads us to conclude that God's future kingdom, represented by the rock, will be physical in nature just like all the others before it. Why would God introduce a spiritual dominion when all the others had been real, physical entities? And how does a spiritual rule suddenly and violently destroy all the physical ones when it arrives?

Furthermore, Nebuchadnezzar, to whom God gave the revelation, would have only understood a sequence of physical domains upon the earth, including the last one represented by the rock that comes crashing to earth out of heaven. He could not have possibly comprehended a spiritual, immaterial one, nor would that have impressed him in any way. *God made this revelation to the king in way he would understand once Daniel interpreted it for him.*

God's purpose was not only to show King Nebuchadnezzar the future, but to demonstrate that His kingdom would someday not only be greater than his, but superior to all the other world powers that would come after Babylon.

Daniel's Vision of Four Beasts

Several decades after Daniel interpreted Nebuchadnezzar's dream, the prophet saw "four great beasts" in a night vision that also represented four kingdoms of antiquity. Of interest for our discussion is the fourth beast or world power, which is the Roman Empire (see Daniel 7:13).

In Daniel 7:7, the prophet describes this creature as "terrifying and dreadful and exceedingly strong.... It had great iron teeth; it devoured and broke in pieces and stamped what was left with its feet." Bible scholar and author John Walvoord wrote that the fourth dreadful beast provides an apt description of the fourth kingdom it represents:

> The Roman empire was ruthless in its destruction of civilizations and peoples, killing captives by the thousands and selling them into slavery by the hundreds of thousands.[18]

The Daniel 7 passage adds a prophecy about a final horn, or king, that will arise during the last and phase of the Roman Empire represented by ten kings (vv. 24–26). This future ruler is the Antichrist, whom Paul wrote about in 2 Thessalonians 2:3–10. Jesus will destroy this blasphemous "man of lawlessness" at His Second Coming by throwing him into the lake of fire (Daniel 7:11; 2 Thessalonians 2:8; Revelation 19:19–20).

After abolishing this wicked ruler (see Daniel 7:25), the prophet tells us that "one like the son of man" will set up His kingdom and rule over the nations of the world (Daniel 7:13–14, 27). Notice the wording of Daniel 7:14:

> And to him was given dominion and glory and a kingdom, that all peoples, nations, and languages should serve him; his dominion is an everlasting dominion, which shall not pass away, and his kingdom one that shall not be destroyed.

Daniel describes the coming realm of the "Son of Man" as something tangible, physical in nature, impacting "all peoples" and "nations."

During His trial before Caiaphas and the Sanhedrin, Jesus identified Himself as the "Son of Man" referred to in Daniel 7:13–14 (Matthew 26:64). Jesus knew that at His return to the earth, His kingdom will include "all peoples, nations, and languages."

Isaiah's Kingdom Prophecies

The prophet Isaiah also confirms the literalness of Jesus' future kingdom rule. Perhaps the most familiar Old Testament prediction of Jesus' birth begins with these familiar words: "For to us a child is born, to us a son is given" (Isaiah 9:6). Jesus fulfilled this prophecy literally; no one disagrees with this assertion. Christ came to earth as a baby boy born in a manger in the town of Bethlehem.

Isaiah 9:6 continues with these words: "and the government shall be upon his shoulder." Verse 7 adds: "Of the increase of his government and of peace there will be no end, on the throne of David and over his kingdom." Isaiah not only predicts the birth of Jesus as a child, but he also prophesies that He will sit on the throne of David with the "government upon his shoulder."

If we apply a consistent method of Bible interpretation to this passage, it leads to the conclusion that Jesus will one day rule a kingdom from His seat upon the "throne of David." The passage means what it says: The baby born in the manger will someday rule over the nation of Israel. No other interpretation fits with the intent of the author or how the people of Israel would have understood the words in the days of Isaiah.

The angel Gabriel repeated this promise when he appeared to Mary (Luke 1:31–33). Mary could only have pictured a physical rule, just as everyone else in her day would have interpreted these words from the prophet. Why would the Lord repeat this promise if it meant anything other than how Mary would receive it—that being Jesus ruling over an actual realm from His seat on the "throne of David?"

In chapter 11, Isaiah prophesies about one from the "shoot from the stump of Jesse" (who, of course, is the Lord) who will someday "judge" disputes in total righteousness (vv. 1–5). The Hebrew word for "judge" in this passage is *shapat*, which often denotes the exercise of *all forms of government.*

Ancient kings comprised both the executive and judicial branches of the government (there was no legislative branch). The text in Isaiah 11:1–5 doesn't limit Jesus to being a judge, as one might assume from a cursory reading of the passage, but is another way of saying that the Lord will someday reign as king over all the earth, exercising *all* the functions of an earthly government.[19]

In Psalm 96:10–13, we see this same equating of judging with reigning as an actual king. Verse 10 begins with these words:

> Say among the nations, "The LORD reigns!"

In verse 13, the psalmist expresses Jesus' future rule this way:

> He will judge the world in righteousness, and the peoples in his faithfulness.

To "judge the world" in this context signifies Jesus' future reign as King.

The Spiritual Kingdom of God

Those who believe that God's kingdom is exclusively spiritual point to passages of Scripture where we see this quality of His kingdom. At the beginning of his ministry, John the Baptist proclaimed that "the kingdom of heaven is at hand" (Matthew 3:2). Because the Church rather than the Millennium began a few years later, many mistakenly identify the Church as God's kingdom to the exclusion of its earthly and physical manifestation that John wrote about in Revelation 20:1–10 and we see all through the Old Testament.

Jesus referred to the spiritual aspect of His kingdom in John 18:36:

> My kingdom is not of this world. If my kingdom were of this world, my servants would have been fighting, that I might not be delivered over to the Jews. But my kingdom is not from the world.

The Apostle Paul wrote about our current inclusion in God's kingdom in Colossians 1:13:

> He has delivered us from the domain of darkness and transferred us to the kingdom of his beloved Son.

If these verses were all the Scripture texts that we had concerning Christ's future rule, we might also assume that it will be spiritual in nature, with no physical manifestation. However, many passages in both the Old and New Testament point to a still-future physical expression of God's kingdom via Jesus' millennial reign over the nations.

Alva J. McClain, in his classic work, *The Greatness of the Kingdom*, does a superb job of demonstrating that Jesus' millennial kingdom on earth will be the physical manifestation of God's current universal and sovereign reign. In addressing the issue of how both a spiritual and physical kingdom come together within God's sovereign purposes, McClain wrote:

> For myself, while recognizing the reality of the problem, I am also convinced that the Scriptures offer a reasonable explanation. In one sense it would not be wholly wrong to speak of two kingdoms revealed in the Bible. But we must at the same time guard carefully against the notion that these two kingdoms are absolutely distinct, one from the other. There is value and instruction in thinking of them as two aspects or phases of the one rule of our sovereign God. In seeking for terms which might best designate these two things, I find nothing better than the adjectives "universal" and "mediatorial." These are not exactly commensurate terms, of course, but describe different qualities; the first referring to the extent of rule, the latter to the method of rule.[20]

McClain's words align with *all of Scripture* rather than just a few selected passages. God's kingdom most certainly includes His current sovereign and "universal" rule over all things. The "mediatorial" kingdom, as McClain described it, is the future and—yes—physical expression of this realm over which Jesus will reign for a thousand years and then forever.

Paul describes how Jesus' millennial rule will culminate in His everlasting rule:

> Then comes the end, when He delivers the kingdom to God the Father after destroying every rule and every authority and power. For he must reign until he has put all his enemies under his feet. The last enemy to be destroyed is death. (1 Corinthians 15:24–26)

In these verses, Paul refers to the transition from Jesus' millennial kingdom to the eternal state after He has defeated all enemies, including death (see Revelation 20:13–21:4).

Yes, Jesus reigns today, and yes, He will reign over all the nations of the world for a thousand years after He returns to the earth. These are not two kingdoms, but the latter is what McClain refers to as the physical, or "mediatorial," kingdom of His current spiritual sovereignty.

Camelot Is Coming

The Camelot about which people dream will be ours when Jesus returns to this world and sets up His kingdom based in Jerusalem. Regardless of our lot on the earth, we possess a glorious future as members of Christ's current kingdom. We will experience the utopia so many people earnestly desire but seek apart from a relationship with the Savior. Because we now reside in the Lord's spiritual kingdom (Colossians 1:13–14), we will one day reign with Jesus during His millennial rule over the nations of the earth.

Jesus will sit on the throne of David and rule over the nations from the city of Jerusalem. And the Bible says we will reign with Him. I will go into much more detail about this coming time of glory for us in chapter 24.

8

The Revival of Premillennialism

> Of course, the historical attack on dispensational premillennialism ignores the overwhelming evidence that the church fathers of the first three centuries AD were uniformly premillennial, not amillennial or postmillennial.
>
> ~D. Allen Matthew, *Theology Adrift, The Early Church Fathers and Their Views of Eschatology*[21]

While Scripture alone is and must be the sole source of our faith and practice, the study of church history serves at least a couple useful purposes. First, it helps us understand the historical background behind what we believe. And second, it refutes those who use church history as the sole argument against what we believe. The purpose of this chapter is to disprove those who deny the prominence of the premillennial viewpoint in the early centuries of the church.

Many maintain that the modern-day beliefs in the Rapture and the millennial reign of Jesus began in the late nineteenth century. They use this argument to disparage these doctrines, claiming that no one held them until quite late in church history. Often on that basis alone, they dismiss teachings held by most Bible-believing churches for much of the twentieth century.

Are such claims about church history true? No. We'll dig into the history of premillennial views in this chapter and explore the history of Rapture opinions in a later one. Together, this information will dispel the lie that premillennial beliefs, as described in this section, did not appear in the church until the mid to late nineteenth century.

Noted church historian Philip Schaff said this about premillennialism during the first three centuries of the church:

> The most striking point in the eschatology of the ante-Nicene age is the prominent chiliasm, or millenarianism, that is the belief of a visible reign of Christ in glory on earth with the risen saints for a thousand years, before the general resurrection and judgment.[22]

Despite not agreeing with premillennialism, he nonetheless states that it dominated the first three hundred years of the church.

The following prominent leaders in the early church held to the concept of the millennial reign of Jesus after the Second Coming. They viewed the Millennium as being separate from the Church Age *and* distinct from the eternal state, which happens after Christ's reign on the earth.

Papias (AD 70–163)

Papias, an early church father, adamantly asserted in the truth of a literal, future reign of Jesus upon the earth. Born in AD 70, he sat briefly at the feet of John listening to the aged apostle teach. He later became a leader in the church at Smyrna, one of the seven churches addressed in the book of Revelation.

Although none of Papias' works have survived to this day, an early church historian named Eusebius (AD 263–339) quoted Papias as writing this premillennial-sounding statement:

> There will be a millennium after the resurrection of the dead, when the personal reign of Christ will be established on earth.[23]

Eusebius did not agree with Papias regarding Jesus' future, and he even complained about his strong support of it.

Justin Martyr (AD 100–165)

Justin Martyr, an apologist in the early church, also affirmed a strong certainty of a literal millennial kingdom. He came to faith in Jesus in about AD 133, after which he vigorously defended the Christian faith before his martyrdom in AD 165. In his famous book, *Dialogue with Trypho*, Martyr taught "the premillennial return of Christ and the resurrection of the righteous before the beginning of the thousand-year kingdom."[24]

Below are Martyr's own words concerning the Millennium:

> But I and others, who are right-minded Christians on all points, are assured that there will be a resurrection of the dead, and a thousand years in Jerusalem, which will be built, adorned, and enlarged, [as] the prophets Ezekiel and Isaiah declare.... And further, there was a certain man with us, whose name was John, one of the apostles of Christ, who prophesied, by a revelation that was made to him, that those who believed in our Christ would dwell a thousand years in Jerusalem.[25]

Although Justin Martyr believed that God had rejected Israel, he nevertheless taught that Jesus would rule for one thousand years in the city of Jerusalem. Although several premillennialists in the early church agreed with his view of Israel, they nonetheless interpreted Revelation 20:1–10 as a literal and future prophecy of Jesus' millennial rule on earth. These early advocates of premillennialism did not combine the thousand-year reign of Christ with the Church Age or with the eternal state. Although this seems inconsistent to us today, they held to the idea of a thousand-year reign of Jesus in Zion, based on the Old Testament prophets and Revelation 20:1–10, despite leaving Israel out of the picture.

Irenaeus (AD 130–202)

Irenaeus, a prominent early church leader and theologian, wrote this in AD 180 in his book, *Against Heresies*, book 5, chapter 30:

> But when this Antichrist shall have devastated all things in this world, he will reign for three years and six months, and sit in the temple at Jerusalem; and then the Lord will come from heaven in the clouds, in the glory of the Father, sending this man and those who follow him into the lake of fire; but bringing in for the righteous the times of the kingdom, that is, the hallowed seventh day; and restoring to Abraham the promised inheritance, in which kingdom the Lord declared, that "many coming from the east and from the west should sit down with Abraham, Isaac, and Jacob."[26]

Irenaeus wrote about the Antichrist, the Tribulation, the return of Jesus in the clouds, and the setting up of His millennial kingdom in *Against Heresies*. Although the Romans destroyed the Jewish Temple in Jerusalem 110 years before he wrote his book, Irenaeus not only asserted that someone would rebuild it, but also that the Antichrist would subsequently defile it. In other words, despite his conviction that God had rejected Israel, he wrote about a Jewish Temple that someone would rebuild in the future.

I can't explain what seems to be a contradiction; although Irenaeus thought God had rejected Israel, he regarded the book of Revelation as literal, unfulfilled prophecy and believed in a physical and tangible reign of Jesus over the nations.

Irenaeus' mentor in the faith, Polycarp, was a disciple of the Apostle John and the head pastor in Smyrna when the book of Revelation arrived in the city. It's much more than a little significant that the one whom John mentored in the faith and likely read the book of Revelation to his congregation passed on a literal and futuristic understanding of it to his key disciple in the faith, Irenaeus. Why else would Irenaeus possess such a view of the apocalypse?

If the Apostle John's most famous disciple, Polycarp, had regarded the book of Revelation as anything but future prophecy, he wouldn't have passed a factual and futuristic understanding of the book on to his most famous student.

Irenaeus' belief that Revelation signifies unfulfilled prophecy in AD 180 speaks volumes regarding those today who seek to discredit its prophetic message through allegory or by limiting the book's appeal to the first century AD.

Tertullian (AD 155–240)

Tertullian was an early defender of the Christian faith and a prolific author. His lived in Carthage in the Roman province of Africa. He asserted his belief in premillennialism in his book, *Against Marcion.* There, he affirmed "the literal reality of both the thousand-year kingdom of Christ on earth as well as the reality of the New Jerusalem."[27] Like so many other early church leaders of his time, Tertullian believed in the earthly, millennial reign of Jesus.

Lactantius (AD 240–320)

We see the continuance of the premillennial position in the writings of Lactantius (AD 240–320), an early Christian writer who became an advisor to the Roman Emperor Constantine after the Edict of Milan in AD 313. Referring to Jesus, he stated:

> But He, when He shall have destroyed unrighteousness, and executed His great judgment, and shall have recalled to life the righteous, who have lived from the beginning, will be engaged among men a thousand years, and will rule them with most just command.[28]

In his book, *Divine Institutes*, Lactantius wrote about what would happen after the Second Coming:

> Then they who shall be alive in their bodies shall not die, but during those thousand years shall produce an infinite multitude, and their offspring shall be holy and beloved by God; but they who shall be raised from the dead shall preside over the living as judges.[29]

Lactantius' view of end-time events matches today's premillennial beliefs.

The Beginning of Amillennialism

The roots of amillennialism, the belief that denies a distinct thousand-year reign of Jesus, began with Philo, an Alexandrian Jew who lived during the time of Christ. He admired the teachings of the philosopher Plato, who taught that all matter was evil and only the spirit realm was good.

Much to the dismay of the rabbis of his day, Philo allegorized the Old Testament in order "to offer the Greeks the best of Judaism and the Jews the best of Greek philosophy."[30] Philo reinterpreted God's Word in this way in order to make it comply with Plato's view of the world. This, he hoped, would make Scripture more appealing to the Greeks while at the same time encouraging Jews to embrace the Greek way of thinking.

Philo's symbolical approach to Scripture later became the pattern for a "new school of theological thought" within the church.[31] In the second century AD, two Christian teachers from Philo's hometown of Alexandria adopted his symbolical way of interpreting God's Word. Clement (AD 150–215) "embraced Greek philosophy and maintained that Scripture must be understood allegorically so as not to contradict it."[32] Origen (AD 185–254) purposely used this approach to make the teachings of the Bible comply with Plato's dualism, which only considered spiritual realities as good and regarded all matter as evil.

Clement and Origen dismissed the idea of the Millennium because its abundant material blessings contradicted the teachings of Plato. In this case, human wisdom trumped the words of Scripture.

The ancient Syrian School of Antioch, on the other hand, championed a "literal and historical interpretation" of Scripture. They vigorously opposed Origen's symbolic approach to the Scripture, which, they claimed, "reinterpreted Christian doctrine in terms of Platonic philosophy."[33] As we've already seen, the majority of early church fathers rejected the errant and figurative interpretations of the Alexandrian School, choosing instead to interpret prophecy literally and according to the intent of the author.

In AD 325, the Roman Emperor Constantine called all the church leaders to participate in the famous Council of Nicea. He summoned the gathering to refute the false teaching that had crept into the church during the previous centuries. The Council condemned the teachings of Origen as heretical and affirmed the place of the book of Revelation in the canon of the New Testament, thereby refuting the amillennial teachings of Origen.

As a result of the Council's decision, premillennialism continued to dominate the church until the early fifth century AD, when Augustine revived amillennialism and, under his influence, this view of the end times became the prevailing viewpoint among theologians for more than a thousand years.

Although Augustine claimed to disagree with Plato on several key issues, he nevertheless incorporated the pagan philosopher's scheme of reality into his theology.[34] He regarded Christianity as an improvement on the teachings of Plato, for sure, but that didn't keep him from accepting the dualism of the pagan philosopher that regarded the material world as evil.

Augustine said the idea of a Millennium "would not be objectionable" if somehow "the nature of the millennial kingdom was a 'spiritual one' rather than a physical one."[35] He objected to the thoughts of "carnal banquets," which he visualized might be a part of such a kingdom.[36]

Do you see how the teachings of Plato influenced Augustine's interpretation of God's Word regarding the Millennium? He chose Plato's teachings over the words of Scripture when it came to interpreting prophetic texts that dealt with Jesus' future reign on the earth.

The Reformation (Sixteenth Century)

Luther and Calvin, along with other reformers of their time, returned the church to a literal interpretation of Scripture. Their Bible-based approach restored the doctrine of justification by faith that had fallen victim to allegorical interpretations during the preceding centuries.

Both Luther and Calvin recognized the considerable damage that the use of allegory had caused to the purity of the gospel. Calvin characterized this approach to God's Word as "satanic" because it led people away from the truth of Scripture.[37] Luther joined Calvin in firmly denouncing the use of symbolism as a way to interpret clear passages from God's Word.

Unfortunately, despite condemning the use of symbolism to reinterpret biblical texts, the Reformers failed to apply their convictions to prophetic passages of Scripture. Due to their anti-Semitism as well as the remaining influence of Plato's dualism in the church, they continued to follow Augustine's example when interpreting texts related to Jesus' thousand-year rule in Jerusalem.

Later, the reformers' principles of a literal biblical interpretation became the driving force behind the resurgence of premillennialism that began in the 1700s and continued through much of the twentieth century. As biblical scholars and teachers applied the same principles of scriptural interpretation as the Reformers, they returned to the millennial views of the early church fathers that regarded Revelation 20:1–10 as a future and literal kingdom.

Luther in particular established two key principles of interpretation that later led to the rise of premillennialism in the church. The first was *Sola Scriptura*, which stressed that the Bible alone was the source of our beliefs and practices. The second was "Scripture interprets Scripture." This signifies that we must view God's Word in a consistent manner wherein one text doesn't contradict another. We interpret passages that are less clear on a matter in light of those that might provide insight into it.

In the centuries that followed, these principles sparked the rise and later the dominance of premillennialism during most of the twentieth century.

Dr. Andy Woods put it this way:

> The Reformers, in essence, knocked over a domino. And once it fell, the Holy Spirit raised up others who could go even further and knock over more dominoes—using the same method that the Protestant Reformers retrieved from Antioch.[38]

The Reformation Continues

After the Reformation, students of Scripture in large numbers began turning away from the amillennialism that had dominated the Dark Ages. Rather than interpret prophetic texts in Scripture with allegory, they let the words of the prophets speak for themselves.

Dr. William Watson wrote an article called "The Rise of Philo-Semitism and Premillennialism During the Seventeenth and Eighteenth Centuries."[39] In it, he documents how the next generation after the Reformers began the trend away from the anti-Semitism and allegorical interpretations of John Calvin and Martin Luther and, as a result, biblical prophecies regarding a future restored kingdom for Israel sprang to life.

Perhaps the most well-known premillennialist during this era was Isaac Newton. His study of the books of Daniel and Revelation led him to conclude in 1706 that God would again restore Israel as a nation, after which the Jewish people would build a Temple that the Antichrist would desecrate in the middle of the Tribulation.

Newton also believed that Jesus would return with His saints after this terrible time of wrath on the earth and set up a thousand-year reign. His thoughts closely mirror those of premillennialists today.

At the end of his article, Dr. Watson lists more than forty-five writers who, from 1585 to 1800, expressed beliefs in some form of Jesus' millennial reign over the nations of the earth. He provided quotes from many of these biblical scholars and writers who paved the way for the revival of premillennialism.

Summing Up

It's true that amillennialism prevailed in the church for over a thousand years, a period that included the Dark Ages. But as Dr. Andy Woods asks, "Should the Dark Ages be the standard of correct doctrine?"[40]

The dominance of premillennialism in Bible-believing churches during the latter part of the nineteenth century and most of the twentieth did not happen because of a few misguided teachers. The roots of this widespread revival of biblical teachings began after the Reformation as students of God's Word applied the Reformers' principles of Bible interpretation to prophetic passages in both the Old and New Testaments and rejected the longstanding amillennialism of church.

The return of many pastors and teachers today to amillennialism, in my mind, signifies a step backward in time as well as a denial of what Scripture teaches regarding a glorious future restoration of Israel. This also signifies a return to allegorical interpretations of prophecy that began as a way to combine Platonism with Scripture and, at a later time in church history, contaminated the purity of the gospel.

Isaac Newton once wrote:

> About the times of the End, a body of men will be raised up who will turn their attention to the prophecies, and insist upon their literal interpretation, in the midst of much clamor and opposition.

This day has arrived.

9

The Basis of Hopeful Living in a Lawless World

> Basic to amillennialism is its lack of a consistent hermeneutic. It must abandon the literal hermeneutic of the historical, grammatical, and contextual approach for some degree of allegorization. The amillennialist must supply ideas or concepts that one would not be able to find by simply reading the text. Allegorization, or spiritualization, brings a meaning from outside of a specific text to interpret it rather than basing the interpretation on what is written in that specific passage.
>
> -Dr. Thomas Ice, "Amillennialism,"
> *The Popular Encyclopedia of Bible Prophecy*[41]

Life in the eternal state will be spectacular, far beyond even our best experiences in this life. Randy Alcorn, in his book *Heaven*, does a superb job of expanding our imaginations regarding our future life on the new earth and in the New Jerusalem. We have much to look forward to when the words of Revelation 21–22 ring true throughout the universe. It's then that death, suffering, sorrow, and pain will no longer exist (Revelation 21:1–4), we will explore the new earth, and we will reside in the most magnificent city imaginable, the New Jerusalem.

In the meantime, we dwell amid chaos, extreme wickedness, and increasing violence. The response to COVID-19 has created a culture of fear unlike anything we've ever seen. Riots and violence continue as powerful and wicked forces seek to overthrow America and eliminate the freedoms we now enjoy.

Is our fate a worldwide form of Marxist government that the World Economic Forum describes as the "Great Reset?" Will God judge those who kill our police, destroy businesses, and spread lawlessness and murder on our streets? Will we see the end of the despair and panic prevalent all around us? Will the Lord intervene in our world at all or any time soon? Have we reached a "new normal" with little to no relief from these things on the horizon?

Only premillennialism answers these questions in such a way that calms the anxieties that often bubble up inside us as we make our way through such a troubled world.

Belief in a literal Tribulation and Millennium is not a matter of stuffy theology without relevance to everyday life. It enables us to base our gospel hope on the firm foundation of God's Word. The Bible assures us of God's total control over history. He's not surprised by the events of our day, but long ago told us that such things would happen and lead to His direct intervention in our world beginning with the Rapture and then with the judgments revealed in Revelation 6-18.

Premillennialism alone makes it possible to put the events of our day into a prophetic understanding that not only assures us that things are not out of control, but that the Lord remains sovereign over history.

Because of its supreme importance for us as the foundation of our hope and comfort amid current world events, the points below offer additional support to the case for premillennialism.

We know it is true because:

1. The Father cannot break His promise to the Son.

In Psalm 2:7–8, we read:

> The Lord said to me, "You are my Son; today I have begotten you. Ask of me, and I will make the nations your heritage, and the ends of the earth your possession."

The context clarifies this as a physical rule over the nations of the world in which Jesus rules with a "rod of iron" and dashes the nations "in pieces like a potter's vessel" (Psalm 2:9–10). This can't be a spiritual realm, nor can it refer to the church; it remains an unfulfilled prophecy.

The millennial rule of Jesus as described in Psalm 2 is a biblical necessity because it specifies a promise from the Father to the Son. If Jesus does not reign over the nations as passages such as Zechariah 14 and Revelation 20:1–10 describe, it would signify that the Father has reneged on the Psalm 2 promise to His Son. Such a scenario is totally unimaginable!

Only premillennialism preserves the Father's promise to the Son and assures us of a future kingdom in which we will reign with Jesus.

2. There must be a future Millennium.

Psalm 2:9 describes Jesus' future rule in this way:

> You shall break them with a rod of iron and dash them in pieces like a potter's vessel.

Some versions have the word "rule" rather than "break." Either way, does this describe Jesus' headship over the church today or something that He fulfilled with His First Coming? It does not! This can't be a promise for the Church Age; Jesus doesn't rule over His Body in such a way.

The presence of rebellion and harsh judgment during this reign of Jesus, as we see in Psalm 2, differentiates it as well from the eternal state where sin and death will no longer exist (Revelation 21:4). No other time fits with the conditions of Jesus' rule as described in Psalm 2; it must be the Millennium where Scripture indicates that sin and rebellion will occur (Zechariah 14:16–19; Revelation 20:7–10). Only the millennial reign of Jesus aligns with the conditions described in Psalm 2.

Only premillennialism maintains the nature of Jesus' rule over the nations as depicted in Psalm 2.

3. Premillennialism reflects the original intent of the prophets.

One can't deny the reality of a future Millennium and at the same time interpret the prophetic words of Scripture as the authors intended or in the way the original audience would have understood them at the time. *Only premillennialism maintains the original intent of the biblical prophets.*

Take the words of Zechariah, for example. He prophesied about a time *after* Jesus' crucifixion when a great number of the Israelites would repent and recognize Jesus as their Messiah. Using words that cannot apply to anyone else except those of Jewish physical descent, the prophet pictures a time of great remorse as the Jewish people recognize the one "they have pierced" as their Messiah. They display their deep regret and repentance (Zechariah 12:10–13:1).

Those who dismiss the reality of a future physical kingdom for Israel cannot interpret the words of Zechariah the way he intended.

If the words of Scripture can mean one thing when written and convey an entirely different sense centuries later, then their meaning becomes subject to the thoughts of whoever is interpreting them at a particular time. The use of allegory in regard to future prophecy, so popular among pastors today, erodes both the trustworthiness and the objectivity of Scripture by allowing interpreters to impose their own viewpoint on the text, offering interpretations that have little or nothing to do with the meaning of the words at the time God inspired them.

Only premillennialism keeps the original intent of all of biblical prophecy.

4. Premillennialism matches the eyewitness and futuristic tone of the book of Revelation.

The book of Revelation begins with these words: "The revelation of Jesus Christ." From beginning to end, the book contains Jesus' revelation to us, His church. Unfortunately, many also treat the book as an allegory from which they can pick and choose what is symbolic and what is not.

John's choice of words negates the allegorical approach to the book of Revelation. The apostle uses "saw" forty-four times by itself and twelve times with the word "looked." He uses "heard" thirty times to indicate he was writing down what he heard. The apostle purposely uses the words of someone communicating God's message based on what he both saw and heard. Those writing allegory do not identify themselves as eyewitnesses to actual events, as does the Apostle John all through of the book of Revelation. He repeatedly stated that he was recording future events as he saw them and was writing down what he heard at a future time (Revelation 22:8).

Yes, the apostle employs symbolism and imagery in relating Jesus' message concerning the future. His overriding intent, however, was to tell us specifically what he saw and heard concerning the future, especially during a time of Tribulation that will come upon the world. Jesus Himself confirmed that the words of the book as prophecy (Revelation 22:6).

Only premillennialism interprets the book of Revelation as future prophecy, which assures us of God's coming judgment of the wickedness and rampant lawlessness we see in our world today.

5. Allegorizing Scripture opens the door to heresies.

The allegorical method of interpreting Scripture, which forms the foundation of those who deny the restoration of a future kingdom for Israel and the millennial rule of Jesus, *always* leads to a further erosion of biblical truth and opens the door to heresy. It has done so in the past, it is happening now, and it will most certainly occur in the future.

In order to deny that there will be restoration of a kingdom for Israel, one must relegate a multitude of Old Testament prophecies regarding the future of Israel to allegory. Such interpretations diminish the importance of words in the Bible and thereby open the door for other biblical texts to fall victim to allegory, which negates the intent of the author. This happened during the centuries leading up to the Reformation, when the use of allegory bled over from prophetic texts to those regarding the gospel, diluting its message and necessitating that the Reformers return the church to a sound, biblical understanding of justification by faith.

The Church in the United Kingdom exemplifies how amillennialism morphs into further false beliefs and even a rejection of biblical standards. While I know that many there hold to premillennial beliefs, a number of leaders and pastors in the Church of England have long since rejected it in favor of false viewpoints that affirm amillennialism.

During January of 2020, churches in Scotland and England disinvited evangelist and missionary Franklin Graham to speak because of his views on the LBGTQ agenda. Bryan Kerr, a Church of Scotland pastor in Lanark, said "Franklin Graham isn't the voice of Christianity." The path to such a misguided statement began with allegorical interpretations of prophecies regarding the future restoration of Israel and the Tribulation, aka amillennialism, which later led to this sad erosion of scriptural integrity and outright apostasy.

Once a teacher or pastor treats unfulfilled biblical prophecy as allegory, others come along at a later time and extend the same methodology to other texts of the Bible. If the passages regarding Israel's future do not mean what they say, then perhaps we can take a different perspective on other texts. The response of Bryan Kerr to Franklin Graham is not at all surprising, given that this sequence began with the rejection of Jesus' millennial reign.

Only premillennialism guards the integrity of all the words of Scripture.

6. Allegorizing prophecy redirects the focus of believers to temporal matters.

Those who deny what the Bible teaches about the Millennium and Tribulation believe the next prophetic event is Jesus' return at the end of this age to wrap things up, judge humanity, and initiate the eternal state. They give lip service to the imminence of Jesus' return, but neither they nor those listening to them actually believe it could happen in their lifetime or even during the lives of their grandchildren or great-grandchildren.

As a result, they focus on the things of this world that lie ahead rather than on the matters of eternity. Their plans for the future exclude the possibility of Jesus appearing at any time in the near or distant future.

In contrast to this mindset, a sound biblical perspective conveys a message of imminence regarding Jesus' appearing. New Testament saints waited for His coming with great eagerness (1 Corinthians 1:7; Philippians 3:20–21). They watched for Him to come (1 Thessalonians 1:9–10) just as the Lord had told His followers to do (Matthew 24:44, 25:13). The Apostle Paul believed Jesus could return for him in his lifetime (1 Thessalonians 4:17).

Some amillennialists maintain the Apostle Paul's two-world perspective of 2 Corinthians 4:17–18, but they are the exception rather than the norm.

Only premillennialism naturally leads to a biblical, two-world perspective.

The words of Alva J. McClain, in his excellent and insightful work, *The Greatness of the Kingdom*, sum up the importance of a premillennial outlook on our world:

> The premillennial philosophy of history makes sense. It lays a biblical and rational basis for a truly optimistic view of human history.... It says that life here and now, in spite of the tragedy of sin, is nevertheless worth-while; and therefore all efforts

> to make it better are also worth-while. All the true values of human life will be preserved and carried over into the coming kingdom; nothing worth-while will be lost. Furthermore, we are encouraged in the midst of opposition and reverses by the assurance that help is on the way.[42]

Only premillennialism offers us hope in a world marked by violence and far-reaching deception. It alone makes sense of our world today, encourages us to remain faithful when despair appears to be our only option, and assures us of God's absolute sovereignty over all of history, even our future.

Doesn't this reassure our hearts at a time when deception is king, many of our judges and leaders thwart justice, and the world races headlong toward a Marxist, one-world government? The Bible long ago revealed that all these things would happen in the last days leading up to the Tribulation and Jesus' glorious return to earth and thousand-year reign.

The events around us may surprise us—and often do. However, the Bible tells us that everything is coming together according to God's purposes to judge the wickedness rampant all around us and establish Jesus' righteous reign over all the nations.

Premillennialism does not increase the fears of the faithful as some claim, but alone offers peace in the midst of uncertainty and turmoil.

The Lord's direct intervention in the affairs of humanity will begin with the Rapture, when He comes to take His Church back to the place that He's preparing for us (John 14:1–3).

Section Three

The Path to a Biblical Basis for the Pre-Tribulation Rapture

The ringing of the phone woke me from a deep sleep. Who would be calling in the middle of night? I felt a deep sense of panic as I listened to my mom's side of the conversation.

I remember hearing her scream as she hung up the phone, as well as seeing the tear-filled eyes of those who gathered in our home during the early morning hours. Despite being just ten years old at the time, I vividly recall the sights and sounds following my dad's sudden death as the result of a heart attack.

I felt greater sorrow in the weeks that followed as the full impact of no longer seeing my dad sitting with us at the dinner table took hold. Strange as it may seem, that awareness did not sink in during the days after his death. Everything seemed surreal at the time.

The Lord, however, knew all about my time of grief and prepared me beforehand for the shock of my dad's death.

Several months earlier, missionary friends of my parents asked if I knew about Jesus' return to earth, and then they talked to me about it. They gave me a tract providing details about the Rapture, the Tribulation, the Second Coming, and the Millennium, which I studied intently later that night under a dim light next to my bed.

I now recognize the Lord's hand in using this couple to prepare me for my father's death.

Although I was saddened and more than a little bewildered, I sensed the Lord's comforting presence as He gave me confidence that I would again see my dad. I took a rose petal from the arrangement on his coffin and placed it in my Bible at 1 Thessalonians 4:14–18, where it remained for decades. In this passage, Paul promises that when Jesus comes for His church:

> The dead in Christ will rise first. Then we who are alive, who are left, will be caught up together with them in the clouds to meet the Lord in the air, and so we will always be with the Lord. (vv. 16–17)

I can't explain why the pre-Tribulation Rapture brought so much comfort to me at the age of ten. I didn't understand much about it, but I believed the words of 1 Thessalonians 4:16–17 signified the time I would again see my dad. That was enough for the small boy of my past; it gave him hope in the midst of grief and much confusion.

Now, after decades of intense study and serious consideration of *all* other viewpoints regarding the Rapture, I remain convinced that the Lord is coming for His Church before the start of the seven-year Tribulation.

This expectation changes everything. Yes, we will suffer persecution and affliction to varying degrees in this life, but we will miss the entire Tribulation when God pours out His wrath on the Christ-rejecting world.

We may see violence and chaos grow worse on our streets and perhaps suffer the consequences of living in a world violently opposed to all that Scripture teaches. *However, we rest in the calm assurance that Jesus is coming for us before the Tribulation begins.*

Why am I so positive of this? What follows are the key arguments that have brought certainty to my mind regarding this all-important aspect of our gospel-driven hope.

The first argument for a pre-Tribulation Rapture is premillennialism, which we covered in the previous section of this book. This understanding is essential, because if there is no literal, seven-year Tribulation, then it makes no difference when the Rapture occurs.

Therefore, I will proceed with the defense of the pre-Tribulation Rapture, assuming that premillennialism, as described in the preceding section, faithfully represents God's Word. If one employs allegory as a way to reject Jesus' millennial rule as well as a literal Tribulation, my arguments in this section will not sound convincing, since I depend on interpreting the prophetic sections of the New Testament according to the intent of the author rather than with allegory or any other method. I give much importance to the *words* of the prophetic texts in the New Testament.

10

The Rapture Is Unique

> The Rapture of the Church should not be confused with the Revelation of Christ's Second Coming. Although these two events are the two most significant occurrences connected with Christ's return in the last days, they are quite separate events involving separate participants, as well as different times, purposes, and locations.
>
> -Grant R. Jeffrey, *Triumphant Return*[43]

During the time I attended Talbot Theological Seminary, a man told me he could not believe in a pre-Tribulation Rapture because it meant Christians living in America wouldn't face persecution for their faith. Not only does such reasoning ignore the torture and the killing of believers in many parts of the world today as well as throughout church history, but it also assumes such oppression will never happen in the United States before the Rapture occurs. As I edit this chapter one more time, the reality of oppressive and even violent persecution of believers in America is right at our door and will happen unless the Lord comes for us in the near future.

Kris Vallotton, a pastor on staff at Bethel Church in Redding, CA, voiced another objection to the Rapture in a paper that appeared on social media:

> I will not accept any theology that takes away my children's future and creates mindsets that undermine the mentality of leaving a legacy.

These type of objections to the pre-Tribulation Rapture elevate human reasoning and desires above what's presented in the Bible. The determining factor for all our doctrinal beliefs must be the *words of Scripture*. As we saw, false beliefs regarding the Millennium often begin by combining human wisdom with biblical prophecy, such as Platonism, which significantly diminishes the intent of the words used by the prophets. It's no different when it comes to our beliefs regarding the Rapture.

It's not that we ignore writers and commentators (you are reading my book); they can add valuable insights and aid us in understanding God's Word. However, we must find the basis for what we believe in the *words of Scripture* alone rather than add human wisdom to it.

The matter of the pre-Tribulation Rapture has become more than a little controversial during the past few decades. Not too long ago, it was the dominant viewpoint in Bible-believing churches all across America and the world, but now it's attacked more than taught by pastors; others dismiss its relevance by their silence regarding our imminent hope.

When it comes to establishing the viability of the pre-Tribulation Rapture teaching, we will start by looking at how the Rapture differs from the Second Coming. Is it a unique event that we cannot combine with the Lord's return to earth?

The following points tell us that the Rapture cannot be the same event as the Second Coming.

1. The Place of the Resurrection in the Sequence of Events

In 1 Thessalonians 4:13–18, Paul tells us that the "dead in Christ will rise first." We see this same order of events in 1 Corinthians 15:52; when Jesus comes for His Church, He raises the "dead in Christ" first. The resurrection of New Testament saints happens first in the sequence of events in these two main passages that describe the Rapture.

In Revelation 20:1–4, however, the resurrection of dead Tribulation saints occurs *after* Jesus' triumphal return to earth, His defeat of the vast armies gathered against Jerusalem, His destruction of the False Prophet and Antichrist, the imprisonment of Satan, and the setting up of thrones for judgment. After all these occurrences that might last several days, the Lord raises the dead Tribulation saints from the grave (Revelation 19:11–20:6). During Christ's return to earth, the resurrection doesn't happen instantly as it does with the Rapture; it occurs much later, after a long sequence of events.

Do you see how the place of the resurrection in the order of events differs significantly during the Rapture versus the Second Coming? In the Rapture, Jesus raises the "dead in Christ" *first*, before He does anything else.

It's impossible to merge the two events into one based on the placement of the resurrection of the dead saints alone. However, many other differences exist.

2. The Participants

Not only does the placement of the resurrection differ between the Rapture and Second Coming, but so does the identification of its participants. John tells us that Jesus raises the following at His Second Coming:

> Those who had been beheaded for the testimony of Jesus and for the word of God, and those who had not worshiped the beast

or its image and had not received its mark on their foreheads or their hands. (Revelation 20:4, 6:9–11).

This group represents martyrs from the Tribulation whom we refer to as "Tribulation saints." When Paul writes about the Rapture, he says that Jesus resurrects all the "dead in Christ" (1 Thessalonians 4:16; 1 Corinthians 15:52). It's clear that this applies to *all* believers rather than just the subset of the saints that John attributes to the resurrection of the dead that occurs after the Second Coming.

When Jesus comes for His Church, He raises *all* the "dead in Christ." At His Second Coming, He only raises the saints killed during the Tribulation, which tells us that the Church is already with the Lord in paradise.

The participants in each of the resurrections further distinguish the Rapture from the Second Coming. They cannot be the same event.

3. The Place Where Jesus Gathers the Saints

In 1 Thessalonians 4:17, Paul states that all believers, whether dead or alive at the time of the Rapture, will be "caught up…to meet the Lord in the air." At His appearing, Jesus gathers us to Himself in the clouds and takes us back to the place He's preparing for us in His Father's house (John 14:2–3).

The passages regarding the Rapture don't mention a return to the earth; once Jesus catches us up to meet Him in the air, we go directly to heaven with Him. As Paul says in Colossians 3:4, when Jesus appears, we "also will appear with him in glory." This doesn't refer to any place here below; heaven will be our destination.

The passages describing the Second Coming don't mention a meeting in the air. Jesus arrives amid much fanfare as He defeats the armies of the world in a climactic battle. It's only after conquering the vast army arrayed against Jerusalem that He sends out His angels to gather both living believers and unbelievers for judgment (Matthew 25:31–46).

In the Second Coming, there's no meeting in the air; everyone stays on the earth when the angels gather people to the Lord. With the Rapture, we will meet Jesus in the clouds.

4. The Destination of Believers

Although this may appear similar to the previous point, the destination adds another layer of distinction between the Rapture and Second Coming.

The accounts of Jesus' Second Coming in the Gospels and in the book of Revelation do not include any return to heaven for the Lord or for anyone else involved in it. During Jesus' return to earth, the feet of those alive never leave the ground. The account of the Second Coming in Revelation 19:11–20:4 doesn't include a trip to heaven.

Such is not the case according to the passages from God's Word concerning the Rapture. In John 14:2–3, Jesus said:

> In my Father's house are many rooms. If it were not so, would I have told you that I go to prepare a place for you? And if I go and prepare a place for you, I will come again and will take you to myself, that where I am you may be also.

The Lord promises to take us to where He resides when He comes for us; He doesn't say He is coming to be where we dwell.

The Greek word for "place" in John 14:2–3 denotes a physical residence. Jesus is preparing a *physical* room for us in His "Father's house." Why would He mention actual rooms within His "Father's house" in heaven in this context if He didn't intend to take us there? What's the purpose of mentioning the physical "place" He's preparing for us if it's not His intent to take us there when He comes for us?

In John 17:24, Jesus reveals another reason for taking us to the "place" where He now resides:

> Father, I desire that they also, whom you have given me, may be with me where I am, to see my glory that you have given me because you loved me before the foundation of the world.

Jesus prayed that we would someday be with Him so that we would see the full extent of the glory He had before Creation. Notice that in John 14:3, Jesus says He will take us to be where He now resides, and in John 17:24, He prays for this to happen so we will see the glory He once possessed and now has regained.

Consider again the words of Paul in Colossians 3:4:

> When Christ who is your life appears, then you also will appear with him in glory.

When Jesus appears, we "appear with him in glory"; we depart from this earth to be with Him and witness His exaltation. This is the Rapture!

Jesus is coming to take us to where He now resides so we can dwell with Him. The whole point of Jesus' promise in these verses in John 14 is that He's coming to take us to the place He's now preparing for us.

The Rapture and Second Coming cannot be the same event, because in one case the saints go to glory with Jesus and in the other instance, everyone stays on the earth.

5. The Transformation of Living Believers

In 1 Corinthians 15:51–54, Paul emphasizes the transformation of living believers that takes place at the moment Jesus appears for us. The Lord not only raises saints from the dead with immortal bodies, but also gives imperishable bodies to the saints who are alive at the time. The apostle again highlights the aspect of our new bodies in Philippians 3:20–21, where He promises that when the Lord comes for us, He "will transform our lowly body to be like his glorious body." This is the Rapture.

This varies from passages that describe the Second Coming where we don't find any references to the transformation of living believers. Although Jesus sends His angels to gather the elect, the text does ***not*** say He gives them imperishable bodies. They enter the millennial kingdom in their natural bodies, an absolute necessity for the repopulating of the earth that happens during the Millennium.

6. The Presence of Rebellion During the Millennium

Since Jesus gives all believers—whether alive or dead—glorified, resurrected bodies at His appearing (Philippians 3:20–21; 1 Corinthians 15:51–55), combining the Rapture and Second Coming signifies that no one would enter the millennial kingdom in natural bodies; that would make sin impossible during the thousand-year rule of Jesus, since everyone would possess glorified and imperishable bodies.

Such a premise, however, contradicts what the Old and New Testaments tell us about the Millennium. Zechariah 14:9–19 reveals that during Jesus' earthly reign, people will have the capacity to disobey Him by refusing to go to Jerusalem to worship. Why would Jesus need to rule over the nations "with a rod of iron" during the Millennium (Psalm 2:9) if everyone has a sinless and immortal body? Who would rebel at the end of Jesus' thousand-year reign (Revelation 20:7–10) if everyone enters the Millennium as a glorified saint incapable of sinning or even reproducing?

The Rapture must happen long before the Second Coming takes place to allow time for people to come to faith in the Savior and survive the Tribulation. The number of those who remain alive will be relatively small, but they will repopulate the entire earth during the Millennium with lifespans similar to those before Noah's Flood.

American pastor and author John MacArthur describes the critical distinction between the two events:

> If God raptures and glorifies all believers just prior to the inauguration of the millennial kingdom (as a posttribulational Rapture demands), no one would be left to populate and propagate the earthly kingdom of Christ promised to Israel. It is not within the Lord's plan and purpose to use glorified individuals to propagate the earth during the Millennium. Therefore, the Rapture needs to occur earlier so that after God has raptured all believers, He can save more souls—including Israel's remnant—during the seven-year Tribulation. Those people can then enter the millennial kingdom in earthly form.[44]

The sin and rebellion that occur during the Millennium can only happen if people enter it with their natural bodies. This means a significant amount of time must transpire between the Rapture and Second Coming; the two events absolutely cannot take place in close chronological proximity.

7. The Rapture Is a Mystery

In 1 Corinthians 15:51, the Apostle Paul begins his discussion of the Rapture with these words: "Behold! I tell you a mystery." Several years ago, my wife and I saw the movie *Murder on the Orient Express*, an excellent portrayal of the novel written by Agatha Christie. The story is a mystery; viewers don't know who murdered the man on the train until the end of the movie. This is what we typically think of when we hear that something is a "mystery."

However, the use of the word "mystery" in the New Testament differs from this common understanding. Instead, it designates new revelation, a truth God did not fully reveal in the Old Testament but later did through His apostles. When Paul introduces the Lord's return for His Church in the book of 1 Thessalonians, he says, "For this we declare to you by a word from the Lord" (4:15). This signified new revelation regarding the prominent place of the "dead in Christ" during the Rapture.

The Second Coming was not a "mystery" during New Testament times. We find an abundance of references to it throughout the Old Testament, and Jesus referred to it often during His earthly ministry. Jude tells us that God revealed the glory of Christ's return earth to Enoch, who lived before the Flood (see Jude 14–15). It is certainly *not* a "mystery" in the New Testament use of the word.

The Second Coming wasn't a new revelation for the church. The specifics of the Rapture, however, do qualify it as a mystery, which the apostles further clarified in what they wrote.

8. The Differing Emphasis of Each

The emphasis of the Second Coming is judgment; during that event, Jesus destroys the armies gathered against Him, throws the Antichrist and False Prophet into the lake of fire, locks up Satan for a thousand years, and gathers those who survive the Tribulation before His throne for judgment (Revelation 19:19–20:4).

The message of the Rapture, however, is one of comfort and encouragement (1 Thessalonians 4:18, 5:11). In 1 Corinthians 15:58, the Apostle Paul offers these words of encouragement based on Jesus' return for His Church:

> Therefore, my beloved brothers, be steadfast, immovable, always abounding in the work of the Lord, knowing that in the Lord your labor is not in vain.

Our instant departure from earth will signify judgment for the world, but for those of us in Christ, it constitutes our joyous anticipation and comforting hope.

The uniqueness of the Rapture, as demonstrated by the above

differences between it and the Second Coming, does not by itself confirm a pre-Tribulation Rapture, but it does require that it happens at some point before the Lord's return to earth. A significant separation of time must exist between the events to allow for people to come to saving faith in Christ, survive the Tribulation, and enter the Millennium in their natural bodies.

11

The Imminence of Jesus' Appearing

> The real issue, as pretribulationists state it, is that the hope offered them in the New Testament is the hope of the rapture before the tribulation, not the hope of survival through the tribulation. Thus, when the rapture is presented without any detailed events preceding it, the fulfillment of the hope of the rapture is properly regarded as an imminent event that *must* occur before the detailed prophecies leading up to Christ's return to set up His kingdom.
>
> -John F. Walvoord, *The Blessed Hope and the Tribulation*[45]

A GEICO commercial from a few years ago portrays a spy on a large, flat roof fleeing from armed men as a black helicopter approaches from the air, presumably to join the chase. The man's phone rings as his adversaries appear ready to capture him and perhaps kill him. Thinking the call is from those coming to rescue him, he answers the phone, shouting, "Where are you?"

We then see his mom relaxing by a swimming pool as she calmly talks to him about his dad's battle with squirrels in the attic as we see the furry animals flee the house and run around the water. As she continues talking to her exasperated son, the narrator interjects, "If you're a mom, you call at the worst time. It's what you do."

Reflecting on New Testament teaching regarding Jesus' imminent appearing, we might change this to: "Once we receive the Lord's gift of eternal life, we live in expectancy of Jesus' imminent return. It's what we do."

When we say that Jesus' appearing is "imminent," we mean that, *from our perspective*, the Rapture can happen at any moment. The Bible doesn't tell us of any prophetic event that must precede the Rapture. This differs greatly from the Second Coming, which occurs after the many judgments and events of the Tribulation (Matthew 24:15–29; Revelation 6–19).

Does the New Testament reflect the imminence of Jesus' return? Yes, we see excited expectation of it in many of its prophetic texts.

It's What We Do

New Testament passages that refer to Jesus' return for His Church have one prominent theme in common: They characterize it as the eager anticipation of the saints. In one way or another, the references to the Rapture reflect the continual watchfulness and readiness Jesus commanded of His followers in Matthew 24:36–44.

Notice how the Apostle Paul describes the conversion of the believers in Thessalonica:

> For they themselves [believers in the surrounding area] report concerning us the kind of reception we had among you, and how you turned to God from idols to serve the living and true God, and to wait for his Son from heaven, whom he raised from the dead, Jesus who delivers us from the wrath to come. (1 Thessalonians 1:9–10)

For these new converts, turning away from idols to serve God naturally led to an excited anticipation of the Lord's appearing. After putting their faith in the Lord, they settled into the posture of enthusiastically watching for Jesus to appear, which tells us that they believed it could happen at any moment—certainly in their lifetime.

In Philippians 3:20–21 Paul wrote:

> But our citizenship is in heaven, and from it we await a Savior, the Lord Jesus Christ, who will transform our lowly body to be like his glorious body, by the power that enables him to subject all things to himself.

The Greek word for "await" in verse 20 points to an "intense anticipation" or an "excited expectation" of a future event.[46]

Luke used the same Greek word for "await" in Acts 17:16 to describe Paul's restless "waiting" in Athens for Silas and Timothy to rejoin him. After the apostle's distressing experiences in Philippi, Thessalonica, and Berea, we know he intently watched and longed for a reunion with his fellow laborers. *This is the same passionate yearning of the soul with which the apostle characterizes the waiting of the Philippians for the Lord's appearing.*

Paul's description of the saints at Philippi anticipating the Rapture only makes sense if it can occur at any moment. If all or even a part of the Tribulation must happen before the Rapture, they wouldn't have had the same attitude, since much suffering and death would, of necessity, have preceded it.

In 1 Corinthians 1:7, Paul used the same Greek word for "wait" as he did in Philippians 3:20 to indicate his readers' heartfelt longing for Jesus' appearing, "so that you are not lacking in any spiritual gift, as you wait for the revealing of our Lord Jesus Christ." Despite the immaturity of the saints in Corinth, they excitedly awaited Jesus' return for them.

This heightened expectation of the early followers of Jesus tells us they regarded the Rapture as imminent. No other explanation fits with their anticipation of it possibly occurring in the immediate future.

We see a similar expression of such watchfulness in Titus 2:11–13:

> For the grace of God has appeared, bringing salvation for all people, training us to renounce ungodliness and worldly passions, and to live self-controlled, upright, and godly lives in the present age, waiting for our blessed hope, the appearing of the glory of our great God and Savior Jesus Christ.

Upon turning to Jesus, New Testament saints began waiting for their "blessed hope," the Lord's return for them, as though it could occur at any time. Such anticipation flowed from their reception of the gospel message. Paul and the other apostles did not divorce the Rapture from their preaching; they proclaimed it along the other essentials such as Jesus' death on the cross on our behalf, His burial, and His resurrection.

Peter wrote:

> Therefore, preparing your minds for action, and being sober-minded, set your hope fully on the grace that will be brought to you at the revelation of Jesus Christ. (1 Peters 1:13)

The instruction of the Apostle Peter in the above verse fits well with the imminent expectation of the Rapture we see in the epistles of Paul.

The writer of Hebrews says:

> So Christ, having been offered once to bear the sins of many, will appear a second time, not to deal with sin but to save those who are eagerly waiting for him. (Hebrews 9:28)

The writer characterizes followers of Jesus as "those who are eagerly waiting for him."

Please understand that the above verse doesn't limit the Rapture to those watching for it, but rather it expresses the eager anticipation that described believers in the early days of the church so much so that it became an identifying trait of them. When Jesus comes for His followers, all the saints will go with Him to His "Father's house."

Maranatha

In 1 Corinthians 16:22, Paul prayed, "Our Lord, come." The word for this phrase in the original text is the Aramaic *maranatha*. This signifies "a petition to Christ that He should return now—at any moment. Paul used it in this letter to Greek-speaking (mostly Gentile) Christians in Corinth because it expressed an idea that had become universal in the early church. Christ could come at any moment, and Christians called upon him to do so."[47]

Jesus' return for His Church was not only something these early saints believed might happen at any moment; they prayed for it to happen *soon*. *Maranatha* expressed their heartfelt desire for Christ to appear take them away from the earth. Why would they pray for Jesus to come if they didn't believe it could occur in their lifetime? *This prayer speaks to the imminent hope they cherished for Jesus' appearing.*

The Didache

The *Didache*, which means "teaching" in the Greek, is a brief document from the early church. Scholars date it to the first century, perhaps as early as AD 70, although its author likely didn't compile it as formal document until about AD 300. Many believe it represents beliefs from the time of the apostles—and some regarded it as inspired—but the church later rejected its inclusion in the New Testament.

The first sentence of the treatise provides an extended title: "The

Lord's Teaching Through the Twelve Apostles to the Nations," and in chapter 16 we find this instruction:

> Watch for your life's sake. Let not your lamps be quenched, nor your loins unloosed; but be ready, for you know not the hour in which our Lord will come.

This indicates an imminence regarding the Lord's appearing, such as would be the case for someone expecting the Rapture to occur at any moment.

Although this is not Scripture, it provides further insight into the anticipation of early believers, reflecting the same expectation of the New Testament saints that the Rapture could occur at any moment.

What If?

What if Jesus had told His disciples that His return was not imminent? What if He had implied it would be centuries or even longer before He returned? What if, instead of telling His followers to be ready and to constantly watch for His coming (Matthew 24:44, 25:13), Jesus had told them to relax because it would be an exceedingly long time before He came?

Can you imagine the impact of such a message? Would the disciples have possessed the same urgency to proclaim the gospel to the world? I highly doubt it. Would any generation of the church afterward have viewed the Lord's appearing with even the remotest hint of urgency? I can't envision that happening.

What about the motivation for purity that results from viewing Jesus' appearing as imminent that we see in 1 John 3:2–3? If Jesus cannot return at any moment—or anytime soon, for that matter—the Rapture ceases to be such a motivation to live for Jesus or abide in Him.

People would naturally think they have plenty of time to make things right with the Savior before His return.

For the prospect of Jesus' return to comfort as well as motivate believers of all ages to purity, it had to be an imminent possibility from New Testament times all the way to our current day.

Once we push the Rapture to an indefinite future, Christ's appearing ceases to encourage faithfulness, and the things of this earth soon occupy our thoughts to the exclusion of Jesus' return and eternity. Our ultimate hope inevitably shifts to temporal matters.

The perception of the Rapture as imminent draws our focus to eternity! A biblical, two-world perspective cannot happen when we believe that Jesus cannot return in our lifetime.

Imminence Points to a Pre-Tribulation Rapture

Why would the apostles portray early believers as excitedly anticipating Jesus' appearing if the Tribulation—with its widespread death, deadly persecution of the saints and Jews, and extensive destruction—had to occur first? Would this be the case if they believed they would see the terrors of the seal judgments in Revelation 6? It's difficult to imagine that being the case.

That leads us to conclude that the Rapture must occur before the prophesied events of the Tribulation for it to be the imminent event the apostles defined as our "blessed hope" (Titus 2:11–14) and something the early saints eagerly anticipated (Philippians 3:20–21).

12

The Expectation of Being Alive at the Time of the Rapture

> The reason for their grief is not explicitly stated but a general inference can safely be drawn from the context. Clearly some of the Thessalonian believers had died since the missionaries left and those who had lost loved ones were assailed with grief because of their death.... They fancied that those who had departed would miss the blissful reunion, or at least come behind those who had lived until the parousia. Thus their grief was not just a natural sorrow for their own loss but grief for the supposed loss of their loved ones sustained by their death before the return of the Lord.
>
> -D. Edmond Hiebert, *The Thessalonian Epistles*[48]

My wife and I walked into a restaurant one night with high expectations. Someone had told us that it was the best place in the area for Italian food, and had provided us with a gift certificate for dinner there. Perhaps it was an off night, but we left unsatisfied with our meals that evening. As I look back, I wonder if our anticipation of a wonderful Italian dinner contributed to our disappointment.

Expectations have a powerful influence on us. The wrong ones lead to much disappointment, even grief, as we will see with the Thessalonian believers. Before I get ahead of myself, let's look at Paul's initial ministry in their city, which will give us a better understanding of his hopeful words in 1 Thessalonians 4:13–18.

When Paul and his missionary team came to Thessalonica during his second missionary journey, the apostle first went to the synagogue to reason with the Jews, as was his custom. Acts 17:2–3 says that Paul spent "three Sabbath days" telling them about the Savior and exclaiming, "This Jesus whom I proclaim to you, is the Christ." After a relatively short time in the city, the Jews in the city became "jealous" of Paul's success in leading Jews, along with many Gentiles, to Jesus. They formed a mob and forced the apostle to leave the city (Acts 17:4–10).

Based on the contents of 1 and 2 Thessalonians, we know Paul gave his new converts considerable instruction concerning the Rapture as well as other topics related to biblical prophecy such as the day of the Lord, the Antichrist, and the future desecration of the Jewish Temple. As a result of Paul's preaching, they began watching for Jesus to appear as soon as they put their faith in Him. Those in the surrounding area recognized their expectation of that event as a part of their conversion story (see 1 Thessalonians 1:8–10).

After Paul and his team left Thessalonica, the Jews from the city harassed them at their next stop, Berea (Acts 17:13–15). This ongoing opposition caused the apostle to become concerned for the welfare of the Thessalonian saints, so he sent Timothy back to the city to check on the welfare of the converts (1 Thessalonians 3:1–2). The younger protégé of Paul apparently had a lower profile on the missionary team that allowed him to reenter Thessalonica without rekindling the ire of Jews.

The Grief of the Thessalonians

Timothy brought back "good news" to Paul regarding the "faith and love" of the saints in Thessalonica (1 Thessalonians 3:6), but he also shared some concerns. One of the troubling items in his report was that the Thessalonians grieved unnecessarily for those in their church who had recently died.

Paul doesn't say why some of their members had died so soon after he left the city. All we know is that the others grieved for them as "others do who have no hope" (4:13).

Was the apostle forbidding grief? Definitely not! Jesus wept moments before He raised His friend Lazarus from the dead (John 11:35). Acts 20:37–38 tells us there was "much weeping on the part of all" as Paul said goodbye to the Ephesian elders. Sorrow is both a natural and necessary human emotion in response to loss or death. Paul doesn't forbid grief; it's a healthy expression of sorrow regarding the losses we endure.

But what was so unnecessary about the mourning of Thessalonian saints that caused it to catch Paul's attention? Their shortsightedness couldn't have resulted from a lack of knowledge regarding the future bodily resurrection of those in Christ. The apostle who later wrote, "If in Christ we have hope in this life only, we are of all people most to be pitied" (1 Corinthians 15:19), wouldn't have failed to ensure that his new converts understood the absolute certainty of their future resurrection, especially since he gave them so much other instruction about end-time events.

The Thessalonians couldn't have missed the promise of their future resurrection and eternal life, which was a basic aspect of Jesus' teaching (John 3:15; 10:27–28; 11:17–27) and central to the apostolic proclamation of the gospel.

And, if the saints in Thessalonica had doubted the coming resurrection of their loved ones, Paul wouldn't have addressed it as a matter of *ignorance* or *misinformation.* Such uncertainty would have revealed an absence of faith on the part of the new converts, and the apostle would have corrected this by emphasizing the certainty of the resurrection with them, just as he did in 1 Corinthians 15 in response to those in Corinth who no longer believed in the resurrection of the dead.

Rather than stress the certainty of the resurrection in his response to their grief, the apostle gives his readers further instruction regarding the fate of the dead in Christ when the Rapture occurs.

Paul's Response

Paul's response to the lingering sorrow of the Thessalonians reveals that they mistakenly believed that their loved ones who died before the Rapture would miss out on it. They were thus "uninformed" regarding the place of departed saints during the Rapture; it wasn't a matter of failing to believe in the future resurrection of their deceased loved ones but rather one of assuming that the dead in Christ would not participate in Jesus' appearing to take His Church back to heaven.

So, rather than scold his readers for their lack of faith regarding the ultimate resurrection of their loved ones, the apostle fills in the gaps in their knowledge by emphasizing the prominent role of the dead in Christ during the Rapture.

How might this misunderstanding regarding the Rapture have happened?

First, when Jesus initially mentioned His return to take His disciples back to heaven, He didn't bring up the fate of deceased saints (John 14:2–3). Second, the Savior described the Rapture with language reminiscent of a Galilean wedding of His day. (In chapter 18, I present the similarities between these weddings and the language Jesus used to describe His appearing.)

By the time the Apostle Paul reached Thessalonica, the disciples had undoubtedly told him about the Lord's words in the upper room regarding how the Rapture fit with the picture of a groom coming for his bride in ancient Galilee. Seeing the Rapture in this way helps us better understand the great joy of our reunion with the Savior. This comparison, however, leaves out the fate of believers who die beforehand. Dead people do not participate in wedding celebrations.

What if, while he was in Thessalonica, Paul had described the Rapture in the same way, as a Jewish wedding celebration of the first century AD? This would explain the lack of information among the believers in the city regarding those in their midst who had died. They anticipated being alive when Jesus returns for His bride and assumed that their departed loved ones would miss out on the great celebration.

In 1 Thessalonians 4:14, the apostle assures his readers that when Jesus appears, He "will bring with him" those who have died in Christ. In other words, "Those loved ones whose loss you continue to mourn are already with Jesus and will be with Him when He appears to take you home. They will not miss out on the Rapture; they will have a front-row seat!"

Not only that, but the apostle also assures his readers that their departed loved ones will be the first to receive resurrected bodies at the time of the Rapture. In verses 15–16, Paul writes:

> For this we declare to you by a word from the Lord, that we who are alive, who are left until the coming of the Lord, will not precede those who have fallen asleep. For the Lord himself will descend from heaven with a cry of command, with the voice of an archangel, and with the sound of the trumpet of God. And the dead in Christ will rise first.

Far from missing the joy and excitement of the Rapture, the "dead in Christ" will be the first to participate in it; Jesus will immediately raise them to life upon His return.

The missing piece in the Thessalonians' knowledge was the role of the "dead in Christ" at the moment Jesus appears, not their lack of faith concerning the resurrection. This explains the apostle's emphasis on this in 1 Thessalonians 4:15–16 on the primary role of the dead in Christ during the Rapture.

Paul completes the picture with these words:

> Then we who are alive, who are left, will be caught up together with them in the clouds to meet the Lord in the air, and so we will always be with the Lord. (1 Thessalonians 4:17)

First Corinthians 15:50–54 identifies this as the time when we who are alive will receive our immortal and imperishable bodies and join those who have gone before us in heaven.

A Probable Scenario

Below is a probable scenario of what happened.

Paul's initial preaching in Thessalonica resulted in converts who not only turned from idols to serve the "living and true God," but who also eagerly waited for Jesus' return (1 Thessalonians 1:9–10). This and the fact that they didn't need further instruction regarding the "times and seasons" of the Rapture (1 Thessalonians 5:1) tell us that the apostle spent considerable time instructing his new converts in future matters despite his short stay in the city. By the time the Jews forced Paul and his team to leave, they knew all about the Rapture and watched for it as something that would happen in their lifetime.

Because the apostle expected to be alive at the time Jesus came for His Church (see 1 Thessalonians 4:17 and 1 Corinthians 15:52), we can assume the Thessalonians mimicked his anticipation.

Their lack of information regarding the participation of their departed loved during the Rapture tells us that the apostle did not cover this matter during his brief stay with them. At this early time in the church, less than twenty years after Jesus' resurrection, it's possible this subject had not yet surfaced. And the way Paul begins his answer suggests he had recently received new revelation regarding this matter since he had left them: "For this we declare to you by a word from the Lord" (1 Thessalonians 4:15).

When some believers in the new church died, those left behind grieved, assuming their departed loved ones would miss out on the excitement of Jesus' return for His Church. To address their concern, which resulted from a lack of information and not a deficit in their faith, Paul assured them that the "dead in Christ" would be the first to participate in the Rapture. They would not miss out on the joy of Jesus coming for His bride.

The Early Saints Expected to Be Alive at the Time of the Rapture

The heartache of the Thessalonians tells us they expected the Rapture to happen before they died. If not, why would they have been sorrowful when they thought that their loved ones had missed out on it?

If Paul had taught the Thessalonians that the Rapture would happen after the revealing of the Antichrist, for example, he wouldn't have passed on the same anticipation of being alive when it occurred. However, he not only expressed the anticipation of being alive at the time of Jesus' appearing, but he also maintained that hope when writing his first letter to them. Notice what Paul says in 1 Thessalonians 4:17: "Then we who are alive, who are left, will be caught up together with them in the clouds to meet the Lord in the air."

Given his elevated status as an apostle in the rapidly expanding church, it's certain that he wouldn't have survived for even a short time under the Antichrist's reign of terror, especially during the second half of the Tribulation.

Only a pre-Tribulation Rapture explains the expectations of the Thessalonians; they believed the event would occur in their lifetime and lamented the thought that those who had already died in their midst would miss it. They grieved because of a lack of knowledge regarding the Rapture, which Paul gave them in his first letter to them.

13

The Surprise Beginning of the Day of the Lord

> If the Day of the Lord did not begin until the second advent, since that event is preceded by signs, the Day of the Lord could not come as a "thief in the night," unexpected, and unheralded, as it is said it will come in 1 Thessalonians 5:2. The only way this day could break unexpectedly upon the world is to have it begin immediately after the rapture of the church.
>
> –J. Dwight Pentecost, *Things to Come*[49]

A news story about a burglar in Rochelle Park, New Jersey, caught my attention a couple of years ago. In the process of robbing a home, the intruder woke up the couple who lived there. Not wanting the owners to catch him in the act, he climbed out a window and fled from the house.

The thief had previously arranged with the Lyft car service to provide a ride for him; he had left instructions for the vehicle to park a block away from the home he intended to rob. Sticking to his escape plan, he ran down the street and climbed into the backseat of what he thought was his getaway from the scene of the crime. Unfortunately for him, he soon discovered that he had gotten into a police car, which made his ensuing arrest all too easy for the law enforcement officers.

In 1 Thessalonians 5:2, Paul compares the arrival of the Day of the Lord to the surprise of discovering an intruder in one's home:

> For you yourselves are fully aware that the day of the Lord will come like a thief in the night.

The apostle likely had a more competent thief in mind than the bungling one in New Jersey when he compared the onset of the day of the Lord to the unwelcome surprise of finding a thief in one's home. No one wants to experience such a shock, yet the judgments of the Day of the Lord will begin in just such a way for the unbelieving and unsuspecting world.

How does the surprising start to the Day of the Lord take us closer to establishing a biblical foundation for the pre-Tribulation Rapture? Let's dig deeper into 1 Thessalonians 5 to discover the answer.

What Is the Day of the Lord?

The first question we must answer is this: What is the "Day of the Lord?"

Many premillennialists (those who believe in a future return of Jesus after the seven-year Tribulation period to set up His millennial kingdom as described in Revelation 20:1–10) agree on the identity of the Day of the Lord. They believe that it includes God's judgments before Jesus returns to earth, His Second Coming, and His thousand-year reign in Jerusalem, as well as the burning of the earth at the end of the Millennium (see 2 Peter 3:10). All these events fit under the umbrella of what both the Old and New Testament refer to as the "Day of the Lord."

The Day of the Lord includes the Tribulation, but is much larger in scope than just this seven-year period. As Dwight Pentecost stated in the quote at the beginning of this chapter, the Day of the Lord begins with the Rapture and the "sudden destruction" that ensues upon the world soon afterward. The Tribulation starts at a later time with the signing of the peace deal between the Antichrist and the "many," which includes Israel (Daniel 9:27). This is an important distinction in our case for the pre-Tribulation Rapture.

The majority of premillennialists also concur that the "wrath" Paul refers to in 1 Thessalonians 5:9 points to the judgments of God that happen during the Day of the Lord rather than the eternal fate of those who reject Christ. So, when the apostle says "God has not destined us for wrath" in verse 9, he's referring to the "sudden destruction" he mentioned in verse 3 that comes at the onset of the Day of the Lord as well as the devastation that comes after its surprising start. He is not referring to hell.

The word for "salvation" (1 Thessalonians 5:9) in the Greek signifies "deliverance" or "preservation from" an undesirable fate. Because the subject of Jesus' return for His Church (1 Thessalonians 4:13–18) and its timing (5:1) lead into this text, we conclude that our deliverance from the wrath of the Day of the Lord comes via the Rapture. If the Day of the Lord includes all seven years of the Tribulation as well, our deliverance from its wrath becomes a convincing argument for placing the Rapture ahead of the Tribulation.

However, not all premillennialists agree that the wrath of 1 Thessalonians 5:9 includes all of the Tribulation. Many, like me, believe *all* the events of Revelation chapters 6–18 fit under the wide umbrella of the Day-of-the-Lord wrath. If this is the case, the Rapture must happen before the seven-year Tribulation.

Those who say the Rapture happens midway through the Tribulation do not include the seal judgments of Revelation 6 as a part of the Day-of-the-Lord wrath in 1 Thessalonians 5. They describe themselves as mid-Tribulationists since they believe Jesus will appear sometime after the calamities of Revelation 6, but before the other judgments of the Tribulation.

Some with a similar viewpoint describe themselves as pre-wrath. They say the Day of the Lord starts somewhere in the middle of the

Tribulation, but before the earth feels the impact of God's fury. They agree with me on 1 Thessalonians 5:9, but disagree as to the full scope of the Day-of-the-Lord wrath.

Many variations exist among those who claim a post-Tribulation Rapture viewpoint, the belief that Jesus comes for His Church late in the Tribulation or simultaneous with the Second Coming. Some with this persuasion teach that only the bowl judgments of Revelation 16 constitute the wrath of God and thus place the Rapture before them. Others equate the Second Coming with the Rapture—which, as we saw, doesn't take into account the many differences in the passages describing the Rapture versus those pertaining to the Second Coming.

This signifies that if we can establish that all the judgments of Revelation 6–18 fit within the period Paul refers to as the Day of the Lord in 1 Thessalonians 5:1–10, it would confirm that the Rapture must happen sometime *before* Revelation 6, since the promise of verse 9 excludes us from the Lord's wrath during this time.

The next question we must pursue is this: Do all of the judgments of Revelation 6–18 occur within what Scripture describes as the Day of the Lord?

Does the Day of the Lord Include All of the Tribulation?

As we compare Paul's understanding of the Day of the Lord with Revelation 6–18, it's important to keep in mind that the Apostle John wrote the book of Revelation almost forty-five years after Paul wrote 1 Thessalonians. When writing about this future time of God's wrath on the earth, the apostle only had the words of the Old Testament prophets concerning this day and Jesus' discourse recorded in Matthew 24.

I believe the following points confirm that the *all* the judgments of Revelation 6–18 fit under the wide umbrella of the Day of the Lord.

1. Old Testament passages point to a prolonged period of wrath.

The term "Day of the Lord" comes from the Old Testament, which depicts severe judgments on humanity that come with a tremendous loss of life. These references portray a protracted time of wrath that coincides well with the judgments the Apostle John wrote about in the apocalypse. The descriptions of the Day of the Lord in passages such as Zephaniah 1:14–18, Joel 1:15– 2:11, Daniel 7:19–27, Jeremiah 30:5–7, Amos 5:18–20, Isaiah 13:9–13, and Isaiah 24 confirm this similarity to the book of Revelation—not only in terms of duration, but also in their devastation upon the earth and widespread loss of life.

Notice the wording of Isaiah 13:9–13:

> Behold, the day of the LORD comes, cruel, with wrath and fierce anger, to make the land a desolation and to destroy its sinners from it. For the stars of the heavens and their constellations will not give their light; the sun will be dark at its rising, and the moon will not shed its light. I will punish the world for its evil, and the wicked for their iniquity; I will put an end to the pomp of the arrogant, and lay low the pompous pride of the ruthless. I will make people more rare than fine gold, and mankind than the gold of Ophir. Therefore I will make the heavens tremble, and the earth will be shaken out of its place, at the wrath of the LORD of hosts in the day of his fierce anger.

Doesn't this sound like an extended time of horror for those left on the earth? What John witnessed when he wrote the book of Revelation resembles the words of Isaiah 13 as well as the other passages that reveal the judgments of this day.

In referring to Old Testament depictions of the Day of the Lord, Dr. Dwight Pentecost, well-known author and former beloved professor at Dallas Theological Seminary, wrote:

> This judgment includes not only the specific judgments upon Israel and the nations at the end of the tribulation that are associated with the Second Advent, but, from a consideration of the passages themselves, includes judgments that extend over a period of time prior to the second advent. Thus, it is concluded that the Day of the Lord will include the time of the tribulation.[50]

Because the Old Testament passages regarding the Day of the Lord point to an extended period of judgment rather than calamities that occur immediately prior to or during the Second Coming, it leads to the conclusion that this wrath aligns with the judgments that John wrote about in Revelation 6–18.

2. The seal judgments signify God's wrath.

All those who delay the Rapture until the middle of the Tribulation do not include the seal judgments of Revelation 6 within the wrath of the Day of the Lord that Paul wrote about in 1 Thessalonians 5:1–3; 9–10.

Several problems exist with this view.

First, the seven trumpet judgments come directly out of the seventh seal (Revelation 8:1–5). If the seven angels with trumpets signify God's wrath, the seal judgments must do so as well, since they arrive with seventh seal. A direct link exists between the seal judgments and the trumpets.

Second, the severity of the seals tells us they belong with the wrath of the Day of the Lord as described in the Old Testament. The first four seals result in the death of one-fourth of the world's population (Revelation 6:7–8). How can one regard events that lead to the death of more than two billion people as not signifying God's fury? This huge loss of life aligns well with the Isaiah 13 passage quoted above; there God declares that He will make people "rare" during the "day of the Lord."

Third, Revelation 6:12–13 describes the sixth seal in this way:

> When he opened the sixth seal, I looked, and behold, there was a great earthquake, and the sun became black as sackcloth, the full moon became like blood, and the stars of the sky fell to the earth as the fig tree sheds its winter fruit when shaken by a gale.

This bears a remarkable resemblance to how Old Testament prophets Joel and Amos describe Day of the Lord (Amos 5:18–20; Joel 2:30–31).

Dr. Robert Thomas, a professor of mine at Talbot Theological Seminary, wrote:

> The sixth seal, which very probably comes very early in the tribulation, is characterized by "day of the Lord" conditions…. This means that tribulation visitations recorded in Rev. 6:1ff are part of the day of the Lord. If one seal belongs to the day of the Lord, so do the others.[51]

In other words, one cannot say the sixth seal represents Day-of-the-Lord conditions while the previous five do not. The seal judgments of Revelation 6 signify God's Day-of-the-Lord wrath, which means the Church must be in heaven before they start.

3. There is a surprise start to the Day of the Lord.

The similarity of the Day of the Lord arriving as a "thief in the night" depicts its "sudden" and surprising start. In 1 Thessalonians 5:3, Paul says it will begin "while people are saying, 'There is peace and security,' then sudden destruction will come upon them as labor pains, and they will not escape."

Just like the discovery of an intruder in one's home in the middle of the night, the onset of this day will surprise all those who are alive. This confirms that it must include all the judgments of the Tribulation as described in Revelation 6–18. Why do I make such a claim?

Where in the midst of Revelation 6–18 would people alive then most likely believe they live in a period characterized by "peace and security?" Where in these chapters would the wrath of the Day of the Lord *surprise* people who thought all was well with the world? The only setting that fits this scenario the best is before the seal judgments of Revelation 6, before the rider of the "white horse" goes out to "conquer."

Once the four riders of the apocalypse cause the most extensive loss of life on the earth since the Genesis Flood, the further disastrous events of Revelation will not surprise anyone as they did at first, nor will people be saying they have "peace and security." They may not yet recognize the calamities as God's wrath, but they will know all is not well. The additional catastrophes will not take them by surprise as did the initial judgments of the Day of the Lord.

The Bottom Line

I know my preceding arguments sound technical. Please know that although these things seem complicated, they're more than a little important to our understanding of what the Lord promises in 1 Thessalonians 1:9:

> God has not destined us for wrath, but to obtain salvation through our Lord Jesus Christ.

To help clarify, I will summarize why the Lord's promise in 1 Thessalonians 5:9 signifies that we will miss all of the Day of the Lord wrath and thus the entire Tribulation.

First, the context of 1 Thessalonians 5:9 confirms that the "wrath" belongs to the Day of the Lord, not to hell. The promise signifies that we will miss the sudden outpouring of wrath Paul refers to in 1 Thessalonians 5:3. When he promises that believers will miss God's wrath in verse 9, he's referring to God's judgment that will mark the Day of the Lord rather than the final destination of those who reject Christ.

Second, when we compare Old Testament passages concerning the Day-of-the-Lord wrath with the judgments described in Revelation 6–18, we find considerable similarity in terms of duration, devastation on the earth, and loss of life. The Old Testament descriptions of the Day of the Lord closely match the specific judgments that the Apostle John wrote about in the book of Revelation.

Third, the surprise element to the start of the Tribulation confirms the above conclusion. Once the seal judgments begin with one-fourth of the world's population perishing amid wars, pestilences (includes widespread pandemics), and famine, the additional catastrophes listed in the book of Revelation will not surprise people as will the onset of this day. Will people be saying "peace and security" with the world in utter chaos and desolation as the result of the seal judgments? It's impossible that this could be the case after the death of a quarter of the world's population during the seal judgments (Revelation 6:8).

As Dwight Pentecost said in the opening quote for this chapter, the only way for the Day-of-the-Lord wrath to fall unexpectedly on the people of earth is for it to happen immediately after the Rapture. And if it includes all of the Tribulation, this places Jesus' appearing before its start as well. Since the promise of 1 Thessalonians 5:9 signifies that we will miss the wrath of the Day of the Lord, and this timeframe includes all of the judgments mentioned in Revelation 6–18, we as New Testament saints will be in heaven during all of the coming seven-year Tribulation. *Jesus will come for us before the Lord pours out His wrath on the unsuspecting world.*

I believe this constitutes the strongest argument in favor of the pre-Tribulation Rapture. Because the Lord promises that we will miss all of the wrath of the Day of the Lord, we cannot be on earth during the Tribulation.

Did the Thessalonians believe Jesus would come for them before the judgments at the start of the Day of the Lord? In the next chapter, we will see that they did.

14

The Panic of the Thessalonians

> If the Thessalonians had been taught posttribulationism, the beginning of the day of the Lord would have been evidence to them that the Rapture was drawing near and should have caused rejoicing. Instead of this, the beginning of the day of the Lord apparently created a panic in their midst, with the implication that before the false teachers had come they understood they would not enter this period.
>
> ~John F. Walvoord, *The Rapture Question*[52]

No, I haven't taken a wrong turn on our path to establishing a biblical foundation for the pre-Tribulation Rapture. The *panic* of the Thessalonian saints tells us they fully expected the Rapture to occur before the onset of the Day of the Lord, which necessitates the Rapture taking place before the Tribulation.

How does it do that?

To answer this question, we must begin by looking at the crisis that caused Paul to pen his second letter to the Thessalonians. With the ink scarcely dry on the parchment of the apostle's first epistle, false teachers forged a message to the faithful in Thessalonica telling them the Day of the Lord had already begun. If true, that meant they would soon endure the sudden devastation of this day and suffer through its many dire judgments.

The text doesn't specify how this errant message arrived at the church; it only tells us that someone claiming to be Paul, or a member of his missionary team, said that the Day of the Lord had already begun (2 Thessalonians 2:2). The response of these new converts tells us they didn't expect to hear such news; it put them in a state of sheer panic.

Trembling with Fear

The apostle addressed the frayed nerves of the Thessalonians by telling them "not to be quickly shaken in mind or alarmed" (2 Thessalonians 2:2). "The verb *shaken* denotes a rocking motion, a shaking up and down, like a building shaken by an earthquake."[53] To be "alarmed" signifies a feeling of "fright," with its usage here conveying a "state of alarm, of nervous excitement."[54] The news regarding the start of the Day of the Lord had visibly rattled them; it caused them to physically tremble with fear.

Why such panic from the errant message? The Thessalonian believers never expected to hear that the Day of the Lord had begun. They understood that the Lord would come for them before it started, just as Paul promised them in 1 Thessalonians 5:9–10.

They understood Paul's use of pronouns in this passage, verses 3–8, to signify that the wrath of this day would fall on others, as signified by the word "them." They saw themselves as a part of the "us" in verses 9–10 who would miss this future time of terror on the earth.

If the apostle had previously told them that they would endure all of or even a part of the fury of this day, they would have anticipated such news and not trembled with fear. While not the most comforting message that could have come their way, they would have at least regarded it as a possibility. Instead, they responded to the report stating that the Day of the Lord had already begun with surprise and considerable angst.

What Their Panic Tells Us

The Thessalonian saints panicked because they believed they would no longer be earthbound at the start of this day. Based on Paul's previous letter, they fully believed the Rapture would occur before the day began.

Their frightened response to the false message provides several key insights.

First, it tells us they expected conditions during the Day-of-the-Lord wrath to be quite horrific. Earlier, in his second letter to them, Paul described their experience as that of enduring "persecutions" and "afflictions" due to intense Jewish opposition to their faith (2 Thessalonians 1:4). Yet despite their sufferings, the message that the Day of the Lord had begun caused them considerable panic. They dreaded the prospect of enduring that more than they feared the hostility they faced from the Jews.

Some equate the future time of trouble at the hands of the Antichrist with the persecution Jesus told us to expect as His followers (John 16:32–33). The response of the Thessalonians negates such thinking. Even though they suffered much affliction at the hands of the Jews, the Thessalonian saints panicked at the thought that the Day of the Lord had already begun.

Second, their response to the false report confirms that they regarded 1 Thessalonians 5:9 as an assurance that they would miss all of the wrath of the Day of the Lord. Why else would the news of its arrival have put them in such a state of terror? They believed they would miss *all* of this time of horror on the earth.

Third, if the true expectation of Paul's readers was indeed the start of this time of wrath rather than the Lord's appearing, it would have been an opportune time for the apostle to tell them—and us as well—that believers would endure all or a part of this future time of God's fury, but he doesn't do that. Instead, the apostle reminds them of the Rapture and calms their troubled minds by assuring them that the Day of the Lord has not yet started (see 2 Thessalonians 2:1–3).

If they had misunderstood Paul's promise in 1 Thessalonians 5:9–10, he surely would have cleared that up in his follow-up letter. Instead, he reminded them that they would miss the wrath of the Day of the Lord, which, as we saw earlier, includes all of the Tribulation period.

The New Testament never instructs believers to prepare for the Lord's wrath during the last days of human history, but instead reveals an imminent expectation of Jesus' appearing.

Is Belief in the Rapture Just a Desire to Escape Suffering?

Some accuse those of us who believe that the Church will miss the Tribulation of merely desiring a way of escape. I once heard a pastor make this allegation in a sermon.

Do you see how the response of the Thessalonians dispels this popular misconception? They were already suffering severe persecution by those opposed to their faith, yet the prospect of the wrath of the Day of the Lord put them in a state of total panic. They weren't living in ease and comfort seeking to avoid any unpleasantness that might come their way, yet they still dreaded the onset of the Day of the Lord.

Our expectation of missing this terrible time on the earth doesn't rest on what we desire, but rather on the *words* of Scripture. We have the Lord's promise in 1 Thessalonians 5:9–10 that those of us in Christ will miss all of the wrath of the Day of the Lord, which includes the entire Tribulation.

It's not about what we desire; it's about what the words of Scripture tell us will happen.

15

The Departure of 2 Thessalonians 2:3

> What Paul is saying to the beleaguered and bewildered Thessalonians who were deceived by forged letters allegedly having emanated from Paul indicating that the Day of the Lord had already begun, is that they could not possibly be in the tribulation period because they are still physically present on planet earth....the tribulation period itself will not take place until there is first a physical removal of the church via the rapture.
>
> ~Andy Woods, *The Falling Away*[55]

The next argument on our way to establishing a solid biblical case for a pre-Tribulation Rapture may cause some confusion at first.

"What can the translation of just one word prove?" you might ask. "Isn't true that the church has always regarded 2 Thessalonians 2:3 as reference to spiritual apostasy?"

Please don't hit the snooze button; it's important to our building of a solid basis for the pre-Tribulation Rapture that we determine the correct interpretation of this verse.

If the Greek word *apostasia* in this verse signifies a physical departure rather than an abandonment of the faith, this by necessity places the Rapture before the start of the Tribulation. However, most pastors and teachers today believe it refers to spiritual apostasy in this context.

Let's look at the evidence for regarding 2 Thessalonians 2:3 as a reference to a physical departure such as the Rapture.

The earliest English versions of the Bible translated *apostasia* as "departure," such as in a physical exit from a particular location.[56] The translators of the King James Bible, however, changed the previous pattern by regarding it as a spiritual "falling away" from biblical faith. Translators since that time have followed their lead.

Although I've always strongly advocated a pre-Tribulation Rapture, in the past I've been reluctant to regard 2 Thessalonians 2:3 as referring to anything but a time of future apostasy of the church. However, recent study has changed my mind. Dr. Andy Woods' book, *The Falling Away*, became the catalyst behind my shift in thinking. Below are the key reasons behind why I regard this as the Rapture and not a time of future apostasy.

The Word *Apostasia* Can Refer to a Physical Departure

Second Thessalonians 2:3 says:

> Let no one deceive you in any way. For that day will not come, unless the rebellion comes first, and the man of lawlessness is revealed, the son of destruction.

Here Paul assures the panicked Thessalonians that the Day of the Lord had not yet begun because the "rebellion," the *apostasia,* had not yet happened and the world didn't know the identity of the Antichrist.

In his book, Dr. Andy Woods provides considerable evidence for regarding the "rebellion" as a physical departure rather than as a falling away from the faith. He writes that the Greek word "*apostasia* simply means to 'to stand away from' or 'to depart.' Only by examining how it is used in its immediate context will determine what the departure is from, whether it be a spiritual or physical departure."[57]

New Testament writers used the verb from of *apostasia* fifteen times. And, as Dr. Woods points out:

> Only three times does it mean a spiritual departure. The remaining twelve times it clearly means a physical departure. For example, Luke 2:37 says, "and then as a widow to the age of eighty-four, she never left the temple."[58]

The sense of a physical departure is inherent in the New Testament usage of the verb form of *apostasia* as in this verse, which indicates that the noun form we have in 2 Thessalonians 2–3 can convey the same sense

As Dr. Woods points out, it's the surrounding verses and even the writings of the author at the time that determine if *apostasia* refers to a physical departure or a spiritual falling away. It's the *context* that determines the translation.

The Context Confirms a Physical Departure

Does the context of 2 Thessalonians 2:3 favor a physical departure, the Rapture, versus spiritual apostasy? Yes, it does exactly that. Both the immediate and general context of that verse tell us that Paul had a physical departure in mind.

Second Thessalonians 2 begins with the words, "Now concerning the coming of our Lord Jesus Christ and our being gathered together to him" (v. 1). Just two verses earlier, Paul reminds his readers of the Rapture from 1 Thessalonians 4:13–18. The *immediate context* confirms that the apostle had a physical departure in mind. Why would he change the topic to a spiritual departure without an additional word of explanation?

Paul's words throughout 1 and 2 Thessalonians also favor the sense of *apostasia* in 2:3 as a physical departure. The apostle refers to the Rapture throughout both books, mentioning it in every chapter of his first epistle. It's clear that he spent much time with the Thessalonians talking about Jesus' appearing (1 Thessalonians 1:8–10; 5:1) while with them and then he emphasized it in his epistles to them.

On the other hand, we don't see any reference to a spiritual departure from the faith anywhere in his letters to the Thessalonians or in any other of Paul's epistles at this time. It's only much later in his ministry that he even mentions the spiritual apostasy of the church in the latter days.

Paul Is Referring to a Definite Event

The definite article indicates that the apostle has a specific event in mind, one that his readers would readily recognize.[59] If *apostasia* refers to a spiritual falling away, we would expect to find a mention of it in the books Paul wrote to the Thessalonians, but we don't see even one mention of it. The only "departure" they would be aware of is the Rapture. If Paul meant something other than that in 2 Thessalonians 2:3, he would have provided a word of explanation to clarify his meaning since he had changed to a topic not yet covered in either of his epistles to these believers. But he didn't do that. This again tells us that Paul had a physical departure in mind. The only *apostasia* of which his readers would have been aware of is that of the Rapture. They had no framework leading them to assume it meant a spiritual departure from the faith; again, we have no evidence that Paul even talked about this until much later. At the time, he assumed he would be alive at the time of Jesus' appearing for His Church.

Furthermore, if *apostasia* refers to a spiritual falling away from the faith, how do we distinguish it from many such times in the history of the church when it has abandoned biblical teachings? Most of the organized church today has already departed ***far, far away*** from the beliefs handed down from the Lord to His apostles.

Could such apostasy associated with the start of the Day of the Lord be much worse than what's happening today with the church's full acceptance of so many deviant forms of behavior that Scripture clearly forbids?

An Example from Church History

As further evidence that supports this interpretation of *apostasia,* we have an example from early church history of a key leader referring to what we now call the Rapture as a "departure." Cyprian, a bishop in the city of Carthage during the third century AD, referred to it in this way:

> We who see that terrible things have begun, and know that still more terrible things are imminent, may regard it as the greatest advantage to depart from it as quickly as possible. Do you not give God thanks, do you not congratulate yourself, that by an early departure you are taken away, and delivered from the shipwrecks and disasters that are imminent?[60]

Cyprian (AD 200–258) used the words "depart" and "early departure" to refer to the Lord's appearing to take His church away before a time of "shipwrecks and disasters." While this by itself this doesn't confirm the translation of *apostasia* as "departure," it lends considerable support to our interpretation of the term as a reference to the Rapture, our physical departure from the earth.

This Confirms a Pre-Tribulation Rapture

If *apostasia* refers to a physical departure and the context and other evidence *strongly* supports this conclusion, Paul is telling his readers, and us, that they could know that the Day of the Lord hadn't yet started because they remained earthbound. This must signify that the Rapture occurs before the start of the Tribulation, since the judgments of this time fall under the umbrella of the Day of the Lord.

The Thessalonians could relax at Paul's comforting words of assurance. The fact that the Rapture had not yet happened meant that the Day of the Lord and its wrath had not yet started. Paul's message in 2 Thessalonians 2:3 assured them that they would miss this horrible time on earth, just as promised in 1 Thessalonians 5:9. They had not misunderstood.

I recognize that many may disagree with my analysis and maintain the view of spiritual apostasy, which I did for many years. If *apostasia* refers to the Rapture, this adds considerable clout to the teaching that places it before the start of the Tribulation If not, many other reasons exist for placing it ahead of the coming time of wrath.

16

The Identity of the Restrainer

> Our identification of the Restrainer must ultimately be determined by the question, What person is able to hold back the efforts of Satan? To effectively counteract and restrain the personal activities of Satan demands a person, and one that is more than human. Only a supernatural person can truly frustrate the supernatural workings of Satan. This would at once rule out human agencies as well as all evil supernatural agents. Only a superhuman Restrainer can do the work.
>
> –D. Edmond Hiebert, *The Thessalonian Epistles*[61]

The second event Paul offers in 2 Thessalonians 2:3 as proof that the day of the Lord hasn't yet started is the revealing of the "man of lawlessness," or the Antichrist. No one will know the identity of the "son of destruction" until the Lord removes the "restrainer" from the earth (2 Thessalonians 2:6–7). As students of biblical prophecy, we may have an assortment of guesses as to who the Antichrist might be, but we will *not* know his identity for sure before our departure from the earth.

At the mention of the lawless one in verse 3, Paul begins a review of what he told the Thessalonians about him while he was with them:

> Do you not remember that when I was still with you I told you these things? And you know what is restraining him now so that he may be revealed in his time. For the mystery of lawlessness is already at work. Only he who now restrains it will do so until he is out of the way. (2 Thessalonians 2:5–7)

Since the unveiling of the Antichrist cannot occur until God removes the "restrainer," and this also happens at the start of the Day of the Lord, then its identity constitutes another key factor in determining the placement of the Rapture in regard to this day, which includes all of the Tribulation.

Who Is the Restrainer?

Throughout the history of the church, Bible students and commentators have identified the "restrainer" of 2 Thessalonians 2:6–7 as the Roman Empire, an assortment of various other human governments, and Michael the archangel. The problem with all these forces, and numerous other ideas offered over the centuries, is that they don't have the strength to restrain the satanic muscle that seeks to bring Antichrist to power over all the nations.

Most premillennial teachers today believe that the "Restrainer" is the Holy Spirit (thus it is often capitalized) and describe this work as restricting the lawless activity of Satan as the result of His special indwelling within New Testament saints. This fits best with the context and with Scripture for several reasons.

First, it corresponds with the role of the Holy Spirit as Jesus described in John 16:5–11. In this text, the Lord told His disciples the Spirit would "convict the world concerning sin and righteousness and judgment" (v. 8). This work, Jesus explained, would begin with the Spirit's arrival in the world after His departure. The Holy Spirit arrived on the Day of Pentecost (Acts 2) and continues to indwell believers. His unique indwelling presence in us restrains the unveiling of the Antichrist and will do so until He departs, presumably at the Rapture.

Second, although the Holy Spirit worked in the lives of Old Testament saints prior to the Day of Pentecost, His unique indwelling of believers began at that time. If this day marked the beginning of the Spirit's convicting work in the world, then it makes sense that the Rapture would reverse His restraining work.

The Holy Spirit will of course remain active on the earth in bringing the Tribulation saints to Christ. The Rapture will mark the end of His curtailing Satan's ability to bring his man to the forefront of the world. However, the Spirit will remain active during the Tribulation, as evidenced by the multitudes who will come to Christ during this time.

Third, the restraining of the full expression of lawlessness that represented the appearance of the Antichrist requires divine power. Since Satan will empower the lawless one, the Restrainer must possess divine power to resist his unveiling to the world until the appointed time set by God the Father. The quote at the beginning of this chapter bears repeating:

> Our identification of the Restrainer must ultimately be determined by the question, What person is able to hold back the efforts of Satan? To effectively counteract and restrain the personal activities of Satan demands a person, and one that is more than human. Only a supernatural person can truly frustrate the supernatural workings of Satan. This would at once rule out human agencies as well as all evil supernatural agents. Only a superhuman Restrainer can do the work.[62]

The demonic forces currently promoting the devil's kingdom on earth account for the exponential growth of wickedness, lawlessness, and extreme violence we now see throughout our world. The Antichrist, however, cannot step onto the world scene until after the Rapture, until the Holy Spirit allows it to happen. Until then, he will remain in the shadows.

Fourth, Paul refers to the Restrainer in 2 Thessalonians 2:6–7 with both masculine and neuter pronouns. Although this point sounds technical, it's an important factor in determining the identity of the Restrainer. Dr. Robert Thomas, a professor of mine in seminary, explains how this uniquely identifies the Restrainer as the Holy Spirit:

> To one familiar with the Lord Jesus' Upper Room Discourse, as Paul undoubtedly was, fluctuation between neuter and masculine recalls how the Holy Spirit is spoken of. Either gender is appropriate, depending on whether the speaker (or writer) thinks of natural agreement (masc. because of the Spirit's personality) or grammatical (neuter because of the noun pneuma; see John 14:26; 15:26; 16:13, 14.[63]

We Must Be in Heaven Before the Antichrist's Peace Deal with Israel

The identification of the Restrainer in 2 Thessalonians 2:3–7 as the Holy Spirit adds considerable support to the pre-Tribulation Rapture viewpoint because it signifies that the Rapture must happen before the revealing of the Antichrist, which marks the beginning of the Tribulation.

Daniel 9:26–27 says the remaining prophetic "week" of years for the people of Israel begins with the Antichrist confirming a covenant of peace "with many" that will no doubt include the nation of Israel. When this happens, those who know biblical prophecy would readily recognize the identity of the Antichrist. If Satan has not unveiled his man before this time, the signing of this peace accord with Israel will reveal him as the Antichrist to all who are paying attention.

The Church must be gone before the start of the seven-year Tribulation, possibly several months or perhaps longer before the signing of peace deal with Israel.

17

The Absence of the Church on Earth During the Tribulation

> Therefore, since the future hour spoken of by in 3:10 is set in contrast with the present set of believers in the church age, and the future "earth dwellers" will be active during the time period in which believers are said to be kept from, it is clear that John speaks of the time or hour of the tribulation. Therefore 3:10 is a clear promise that Christ will keep believers from the time of the seven-year tribulation.
>
> -Thomas Ice, *Kept From the Hour*[64]

When it comes to interpreting the book of Revelation, controversy rages in the church today.

Some believe John wrote the book in code to encourage first-century believers amid great persecution; they claim it has *no significance* for believers. Others say people living during the first century saw the fulfillment of *all* its prophecies; this makes the book an historical account rather than mainly a prophetic glimpse of what still lies in the future. Yet others teach that the apostle wrote the book of Revelation as an allegory, although they assume a small part of it still awaits fulfillment, such as portions of chapters 21 and 22 (even here disagreements abound in the allegorical camp as to what is literal and what is symbolic in the apocalypse).

Premillennialists alone regard the book of Revelation as future prophecy, the very thing it claims to be (22:6–7, 18). As previously noted, John's choice of words repudiates the teaching that he wrote the book as an allegory with little or no future implication for people today. He uses the word "saw" forty-four times by itself and twelve times with the word "looked." He uses the word "heard" thirty times to indicate he was writing down words he heard.

In Revelation 22:8, John emphasizes his role as an eyewitness to future events:

> I, John, am the one who heard and saw these things.

Those who insist on a mainly allegorical interpretation of Revelation refuse to acknowledge the repeated testimony of the apostle that he was recording events he saw and words he heard. He went out of his way to emphasize that he was writing about the future, but many today ignore his words to this effect.

This brings us the next signpost on our way to establishing a biblical foundation for the pre-Tribulation Rapture: the absence of the Church on earth during the Tribulation.

Jesus Will Keep Us Out of the Coming Worldwide Trial

In Revelation 3:10, Jesus makes this promise to the church at Philadelphia:

> Because you have kept my word about patient endurance, I will keep you from the hour of trial that is coming on the whole world, to try those who dwell on the earth.

One question we must explore is this: Do Jesus' words in this verse have any significance for us today, or were they just for the church at Philadelphia that existed at the end of the first century?

First, many premillennialists believe that the characteristics of the seven churches line up well with seven periods in church history. Todd Hampson, in his book, *The Non-Prophet's Guide to the Book of Revelation*, wrote:

> An in-depth study of Revelation 2–3 and how these chapters line up with church history could easily be an entire book by itself.[65]

Second, Jesus also indicates that aspects of the last five churches will exist at the time of His appearing. Hampson sums it up like this:

> It is interesting to note that letters to the last five churches—Pergamos, Thyatira, Sardis, Philadelphia, and Laodicea—each include statements about the Lord's return while the churches still existed. Elements from these five periods of church history also happen to still be in existence today.[66]

With this in mind, let's explore the details of Jesus' promise to the church at Philadelphia, one that has characteristics that still apply to today. What is the "hour of trial" He says will impact the whole world? This designation tells us it's something different than persecution against believers, since it includes everyone on earth. The entire planet, rather than just a single nation or even a continent, will experience the turmoil of this coming time.

The period of distress that John describes in Revelation 6–18 fits especially well with the coming "hour of trial" that Jesus refers to in Revelation 3:10. It comes within the context of Jesus' promise to the church and it fits the description of an interval that will test the entire planet.

The fact that this testing is specifically for "those who dwell on the earth" further confirms its reference to the judgments on earth we identify as the Tribulation. John uses this phrase in eight instances in the book of Revelation (6:10; 8:13; 11:10; 13:8–12, 14; 14:6; and 17:8). In each occurrence after Revelation 3:10, the description either refers to either people impacted by the Tribulation or to those refusing to repent of their sins during that time.

John identifies those who will endure the "hour of trial" as those who will be alive on earth for the judgments that begin in chapter 6 and continue through chapter 18.

Jesus follows up His words in Revelation 3:10 with another promise: "I am coming soon" (v. 11). The Greek word for "soon" more accurately denotes an event that takes place "quickly." The apostle also used this word in John 11:29 about Mary: "And when she heard it, she rose quickly and went to him." It makes no sense to translate the verse as "she rose soon."

Jesus connected His speedy return with His pledge to keep the church at Philadelphia out of the time of testing for the entire world. Since He hasn't yet returned, His promise to keep the Church out of a worldwide trial awaits fulfillment.

All the biblical evidence we've covered so far indicates that Jesus' speedy return that delivers the church from the coming "hour of trial" is none other than the pre-Tribulation Rapture that removes the Church from the earth before the season of trouble that John tells us will impact the "earth dwellers" who refuse to turn away from their sins (Revelation 9:20–21).

If Jesus intended for the Church to go through the judgments that He was about to unveil to the Apostle John in the upcoming chapters, He surely would have provided some guidance for enduring them in His letters to the last five churches that mention His return. Instead, the Lord promises that His saints will miss the still-future "trial" that is coming upon all how dwell on the earth. We will be in heaven via the Rapture during the judgments outlined in Revelation 6–18.

Furthermore, the Apostle John doesn't refer to the Church even once in his descriptions of the Tribulation judgments. That's because we will be in heaven, safe from the turmoil and devastation occurring throughout the earth.

The Presence of Other Witnesses During the Tribulation

In a radio interview with author and speaker Jan Markell of Olive Tree Ministries on November 7, 2020, Amir Tsarfati, a former captain in the Israeli army and worldwide speaker on biblical prophecy, questioned the need for the two witnesses of Revelation 11:1–13 if the Church is present on earth during the Tribulation. Isn't it the job of the Church to bear witness to the gospel during this current age?

In addition to these two witnesses, in Revelation 14:6–7, John writes this about an angel who will share the good news of salvation during the time of the Tribulation:

> Then I saw another angel flying directly overhead, with an eternal gospel to proclaim to those who dwell on earth, to every nation and tribe and language and people. And he said with a loud voice, "Fear God and give him glory, because the hour of his judgment has come, and worship him who made heaven and earth, the sea and the springs of water."

Why does the Lord need to send an angel to proclaim the gospel to people during this time if the Church is still present? This only makes sense with a pre-Tribulation Rapture and the absence of the Church. Otherwise, wouldn't it be the task of believers to keep fulfilling the Great Commission during this time?

Amir also brought up the 144,000 Jews whom God will "seal" or protect as the world experiences God's wrath (Revelation 7:1–8). Many believe they will act as evangelists. If the Church remains on earth at that point, why the need to give these Israelites special protection so that they may evangelize the world?

Furthermore, sealing a select group of Jewish people doesn't fit with what we read about the Church in the New Testament. In Colossians 3:11, Paul wrote about the Body of Christ:

> Here there is not Greek and Jew, circumcised and uncircumcised, barbarian, Scythian, slave, free; but Christ is all, and in all.

The special setting apart and protection of 144,000 Israelites from the twelve tribes tells us the Church cannot be present on earth; this is a time when God deals exclusively with Israel in bringing His chosen people back to Himself.

The Twenty-four Elders

The presence of the twenty-four elders in heaven, as described in Revelation 4–5, further confirms the reality of Jesus' promise to keep believers out of the "hour of trial," the time of Tribulation (Revelation 3:10–11a). If these elders represent the raptured Church—and the evidence strongly suggests that they do—then we have a description of the Church in heaven with Jesus before the judgments of Revelation 6 commence.

The following points highlight the reasons for this identification of the elders.

First, they sit on twenty-four thrones (Revelation 4:4), which signifies rule and authority. The Bible never pictures angels as sitting on thrones; it reserves the privilege of ruling with Christ for New Testament saints and no one else. Hebrews 1:14 describes angels as "ministering spirits set out to serve for the sake of those who are to inherit salvation."

Second, the word "elder" in God's Word applies to men but never to angels. Since the term also implies an aging process, it cannot apply to angels. Of course, by the time we reach paradise, aging will no longer be a part of our experience.

Third, the "white garments" (4:4) refer to the dress of believers. John MacArthur says:

> Christ promised the believers at Sardis that they would "be clothed in white garments" (3:5).... White garments symbolize Christ's righteousness imputed to believers at salvation.[67]

Once in heaven, we will experience complete wholeness and will wear white robes as a result. The elders represent the Church clothed in Jesus' righteousness signified by their "white garments."

Fourth, the elders have "crowns on their heads" (4:4). Scripture promises crowns as rewards to believers (2 Timothy 4:18; 1 Peter 5:4; James 1:12). The elders later "cast their crowns before the throne" of the Lord, recognizing that their rewards really belong to the One who enabled them to live for Him during their time on earth (4:9–11). This fits with New Testament saints who have already appeared before the Judgment Seat of Christ to receive rewards for their faithful service on earth.

Dr. Thomas Ice sums up the significance of identifying the elders as representing the Church:

> Since the 24 elders of Revelation represent the church in heaven, this means that the church—the body of Christ and his Bride—is complete, since she has received her rewards (i.e., the crowns) and is in a position of co-rulership with Christ (Rev. 3:21). This depiction supports a pre-trib rapture because from a chronological perspective of Revelation 4 the events of the tribulation have yet to begin. How do we know? We know because Revelation 5 presents the plan for tribulation judgment as contained in the scroll that only the Lamb is worthy to open.[68]

Who else can the elders be except representatives of the Church in heaven with Jesus before the judgments of Revelation 6 commence? Their song applies to those redeemed by Jesus' blood who will reign with Him in His kingdom (5:9–10). These words signify the Body of Christ. This points to the future fulfillment of the Lord's promises to the true saints at Thyatira and even Laodicea (2:26–27; 3:21).

The identification of the twenty-four elders as representing the Church verifies our presence in heaven before the start of the Tribulation judgments recorded in the book of Revelation.

18

The Joy of the Groom and Bride

Not only will we see his [God's] face and live, but we will likely wonder if we ever lived before we saw his face. To see God will be our greatest joy, the joy by which all others will be measured.

–Randy Alcorn, *Heaven*[69]

Many in the room, including his wife Carol, believed he would not survive the night. Louis Talbot, the longtime president of Biola University and driving force behind the formation of Talbot Theological Seminary, lay in a hospital bed stricken with pneumonia seemingly at the end of his life.

Seeing the tears stream down the face of his wife, Talbot responded, "What's the matter with you? *For this I was born.* For this I've lived all my life—*to see my Saviour face to face.* It will be all glory. I can hardly wait."[70] He so longed to see Jesus that the thought of dying filled him with joyous anticipation rather than sorrow.

He did not die that night, although for a moment the next morning, Louis thought he was in heaven. "Looking around at the bleak hospital room, he said, 'If *this* is heaven, I certainly misled a lot of people while I was down on earth!' "[71]

While we smile at Talbot's sense of humor, we also recognize in his words that our ultimate hope is also that of seeing our beloved Savior "face to face." This can happen either through death or at the time of the Rapture, which is Jesus' return to take His Church back to his "Father's house" as He promised us in John 14:2–3.

However, many believers today cringe at the thought of the Rapture. Those outside of Christ *ridicule* our blessed hope, and even many who claim to follow Jesus mock it.

What causes people to dread or disdain it? Does the Rapture's possible abrupt intrusion in our lives make even believers fear it? Perhaps people sense that their dreams for this life will vanish before they have a chance to materialize. Why should anyone look forward to such a sudden and unexpected conclusion to their current existence and expectations for the future?

I suspect many of us can identify with at least a few of the reasons above. I've also felt some of these same apprehensions in my past.

Does Scripture give us any insight that enables us to look at the Rapture in a more positive light, as a source of joy rather than apprehension? Is there a way to look at meeting Jesus in the air with same anticipation Louis Talbot possessed at seeing him after his death?

I believe there is.

The Bible pictures the Rapture as an event when a bridegroom comes for his bride. Both Jesus and the Apostle Paul spoke of the Rapture in terms that would have sparked images of first-century AD Jewish weddings, especially to those in Galilee, home to Jesus and His disciples.

As we look at these ancient customs, we see a picture that not only washes away our fears regarding Rapture, but also makes passages such as John 14:2–3 and 1 Thessalonians 4:13–18 come alive with a joyous anticipation of meeting our Savior in the air!

The Betrothal

Jewish marriages in the first century AD began with the groom entering a marriage covenant with his bride. This happened during a betrothal ceremony, during which the groom and bride drank a cup of wine in the presence of both sets of parents as well as in front of many people in their town; this "sealed the covenant" that bound the couple together.

During the Galilean marriage betrothal, the man offered the woman he desired to marry a cup of wine. If she took the cup and drank the wine, that signified her acceptance of the proposal. The act of giving the cup back to the man without drinking from it indicated her refusal. After the bride drank from the cup, the man also drank from it, sealing the marriage covenant between the two. The bridegroom then announced he would not drink any wine from that point until the time of their wedding feast.[72]

In the upper room before His crucifixion, Jesus' actions and words mirrored these wedding customs and would have sparked images of the betrothal in the minds of the disciples. As Galileans, they could not have missed the resemblance of Jesus' words to the betrothals they had often witnessed growing up in Galilee.

As Jesus gave the disciples the cup, He said, "Drink of it, all of you, for this is my blood of the covenant, which is poured out for the forgiveness of sins" (Matthew 26:27b–28). Yes, this referred to the New Covenant of which Jeremiah and Ezekiel wrote, but it also symbolized the Church as the Bride of Christ and His betrothal to her. The drinking of the wine by the disciples and Jesus signified the engagement of the Church to the Savior.

Jesus then said to His disciples, "Truly, I say to you, I will not drink again of the fruit of the vine until that day when I drink it new in the kingdom of God" (Mark 14:25; see also Luke 22:18 and Matthew

26:29). By repeating the exact words that a groom would say at the betrothal ceremony, Jesus emphasized His role as the groom and the disciples, representing the Church, as the bride.

The Preparation of a Room for the Bride

After the bridegroom confirmed the marriage covenant with his bride, the couple lived apart until the day he came to take her back to his father's house. In the meantime, they both kept busy with preparations for the wedding.

The groom had two tasks to perform. His biggest undertaking consisted of building a room for the couple within his father's house. In a typical Galilean village of Jesus' day, many homes had several additions where grooms had added rooms to serve as bridal chambers for the couple when their wedding day arrived.[73] The groom's other responsibility was preparing food for the wedding feast to be held on the night he brought his bride to his father's house.

At the completion of the betrothal, the groom announced his intention to prepare a room for his bride just as Jesus did in John 14:2–3:

> In my Father's house are many rooms. If it were not so, would I have told you that I go to prepare a place for you? And if I go and prepare a place for you, I will come again and will take you to myself, that where I am you may be also.

These words certainly would have sparked images of Jewish wedding customs in the minds of the disciples. To calm their fears regarding His departure, Jesus assured them that, just like the Jewish bridegrooms of their day, He would prepare rooms for them in His Father's house and come back to take them there.

The Father Determined the Timing

According to ancient Galilean customs, the father of the bridegroom decided when his son had successfully completed his work on the room and finished his preparations for the wedding feast. He alone determined the day and hour when he would tell his son to go get his bride.[74]

In Matthew 24:3,6 Jesus said:

> But concerning that day and hour no one knows, not even the angels of heaven nor the Son, but the Father only.

When the disciples heard these words, they would have immediately connected them to the wedding customs of their day. The Lord's response to His disciples in Acts 1:7 would also have reminded them again of the Father's sovereignty in determining the timing of His return for them.

The Surprise Return of the Groom

When the time came, the father of the groom typically woke up his son in the middle of the night and told him to go get his bride. The groom then gathered his friends and set out together for the woman's home.

> The bridegroom would abduct his bride secretly, like a thief at night, and take her to the wedding chamber. As the bridegroom approached the bride's home, he would shout and blow the shofar (ram's horn trumpet) so that she had some warning to gather her belongings to take into the wedding chamber. The bridegroom and his friends would come into the bride's house and get the bride and her bridesmaids.[75]

After hearing the loud fanfare outside, the bride appeared outside her home along with her bridesmaids, all dressed in wedding clothes, which they typically slept in for days or even weeks in anticipation of this moment.

The bride then stepped into a litter; those accompanying the groom then *lifted her off the ground and carried her to the home of the groom.*[76] Doesn't this sound like what happens in 1 Thessalonians 4:17, where we read that the Lord catches us up to meet Him in the air? Just as the Jewish brides of the first century, Jesus will pick us up and carry us to the place He is preparing for us in His Father's house. The resemblance couldn't be any more remarkable.

According to first-century AD Galilean traditions, the wedding party and some town folk joined in a feast at the home of the groom once the bride and groom arrived. The loud fanfare of the groom coming for his bride likely woke up many in the town.

Seven Days

After an initial celebration, the couple entered the bridal chamber, where they remained isolated for seven days.

> Once fetched, the two returned to the groom's father's house where they were secluded in a bridal chamber (huppah). While inside the chamber they consummated their marriage by entering physical union for the first time. They remained secluded in the chamber for seven days while the wedding guests enjoyed the wedding feast at the groom's father's house.[77]

This fits rather well with a pre-Tribulation Rapture, doesn't it? Rather than seven days, however, the Church will spend seven years with the Lord while those left behind will go through the horrors of the Tribulation. It's easy to make the comparison of seven days with the seven years of judgments described in Revelation 6–18.

The Wedding Celebration

After the seven days in seclusion, the couple emerged for another celebration. Jesus and His disciples attended such an occasion in Cana (John 2:1–12). Although few details of these feasts have survived to this day, we know they could last up to a week. Revelation 19:6–8 tells us about the "marriage supper of the Lamb" in heaven. Some place this celebration on earth after the Second Coming, but most believe it will occur just before Jesus' return to earth.

The Comforting Message Regarding the Rapture

The brides of Jesus' day did not fear the sudden arrival of their bridegroom. They looked forward to it with great expectation; it was perhaps the most exciting aspect of their romance. The anticipation would have filled the bride's heart with much joy as she awaited the groom's arrival to whisk her away to the "place" he had prepared for her.

This way of looking at the Rapture gives us much comfort because:

1. He is preparing a place for us!

The "place" of which Jesus spoke in John 14:2–3 signifies a specific physical location. Jesus is preparing a "place" for us, and we can be sure it will be incredible. It's difficult to envision what this might be like, but I believe our "room," or perhaps a suite, will have many perks signifying Christ's great love for us.

The certainty that Jesus is coming to take us back to heaven, to paradise, should be a cause for joy rather than fear. As the grooms in Jesus' day prepared places for their brides, we can imagine they did so with a heart full of love. Isn't Jesus feeling the same love for us, His Bride?

2. The Rapture is our Groom returning for us, His Bride!

Although the suddenness inherent in the Rapture alarms us at times, it helps to consider that this comprised the excitement and romance of Jewish marriages of the first century AD. The groom did not come to harm his bride; quite the contrary: he came to *carry* her to the room he had lovingly prepared for her. It was a cause for feasting and celebration rather than dread.

Everything in these customs speaks of the great love of the groom for his bride and thus to the even greater love of Christ for us, His Bride! He can hardly wait for the day the Father tells Him to "go get your bride." Oh, the joy that will be on Jesus' face when we see Him on that glorious day! He will want to celebrate just as much as we will.

3. The Rapture will lead to celebration!

Once the bride and groom finished their seven days in seclusion, they celebrated! They, along with their attendants, friends, and invited guests came together for a feast. Such a festal celebration lies in our future as well. Revelation 19:6–10 describes the Marriage Supper of the Lamb.

We will be together with the New Testament saints of all the ages, including saved family and friends who have died before us, and feast with our Redeemer. The wedding dinners and dances of our day last several hours at best. I believe this feast might last for weeks. If those of the first century AD could last up to a week, it seems fair to assume ours will last at least that long and likely much longer.

4. The imagery that presents the Rapture as a groom coming for his bride argues strongly for a pre-Tribulation Rapture.

The picture that Jesus gave His disciples concerning His return for them depicts a pre-Tribulation Rapture. The preparing of a place for us, the sudden and unexpected return, and the seven days in the bridal chamber are just a few aspects of the first-century Jewish wedding customs that accurately foreshadow a Rapture before the start of the Tribulation.

5. The alternative should scare us, not the Rapture!

During the seven years we are with Jesus in heaven, the Tribulation will ravage people on earth. The Day of the Lord will be a time of tremendous suffering and widespread destruction and death upon the earth. Billions of people will perish as the result of famines, earthquakes, wars, pandemics, and other judgments.

The prospect of living on earth while this is going on, not the Rapture, should terrify us.

Many will turn to the Savior, but most of those who do won't survive to the end of the Tribulation because of the intense persecution generated by the Antichrist.

We will be much, much better off with the Lord than we would if we remained on the earth during the seven devastating years of the Tribulation. Jesus is coming to lovingly take us out of this world before this widespread destruction and death. Whenever you think of the Rapture, please remember the terror of what those left behind will experience.

The Rapture is just as much a rescue operation as it is an act of Jesus' supreme love for Hs Bride. He will not leave us behind to endure the horrible judgments of the Day of the Lord. The joy of seeing Him and the place He has prepared for us will far exceed any wish to be back on earth.

19

The Evidence from Church History

> A more cogent explanation is that pretribulationism arose as a refinement of premillennialism based on literal interpretation of prophecy which made it difficult to harmonize the doctrine of the rapture with the second coming of Christ to set up his kingdom. Most pretribulationists obviously base their views on the Bible, not on the historic background of the doctrine.
>
> ~John F. Walvoord, *The Blessed Hope and the Tribulation*[78]

"The pre-Tribulation Rapture cannot possibly be true, because no one believed in it until 150 years ago." I hear or read similar statements almost every week.

Those who mock our beliefs in this way make two critical errors. First, they base their denials of a Rapture on church history rather than on the words of Scripture. Second, the claim that the belief in pre-Tribulation Rapture originated 150 years ago with John Darby is demonstrably false.

Please understand that the purpose of this chapter is *not* to justify my belief in the pre-Tribulation Rapture based on history. Scripture alone is the basis for what I believe. Rather, I seek to provide *evidence* of a belief in the Rapture from the early centuries of the church. The first matter I need to clarify is the origin of this word, which many people say does not appear in Scripture.

Where Did We Get the Word "Rapture"?

Since many people object to our use of the word "Rapture" because it doesn't appear on the pages of the Bible, it's necessary to understand its origin. It comes from a Latin translation of the Bible from about AD 400 called the Vulgate. The Vulgate uses the Latin word *rapturo* to translate the Greek word *harpazo* in 1 Thessalonians 4:17.

The words "caught up" in our English translations capture the essence of the Greek *harpazo* just as the Latin *rapturo* did when Jerome and others translated the Bible into Latin.

Starting sometime in the late 1800s, Bible teachers began using the word "Rapture" to describe the event Paul wrote about in 1 Thessalonians 4:13–18 as well as in 1 Corinthians 15:50–56 and Philippians 3:20–21. These students of Scripture chose a word, based on the ancient Latin translation of the Bible, to describe the event that the apostle wrote about in these texts and several others. They applied a label to what Jesus first mentioned in John 14:2–3 and the apostles later described with much greater detail; they did not create a new event. They merely separated Jesus' appearing for His Church from the Second Coming and assigned it the designation of "Rapture."

With this understanding, let's move into the realm of church history, where we find many instances of the belief in a Rapture followed by a period of Tribulation before the Second Coming. We will begin with Irenaeus, a prominent leader and theologian during the second century AD.

Irenaeus (AD 130–202)

In AD 180, Irenaeus wrote *Against Heresies* to refute the errors of Gnosticism, which posed a great threat to the church at the time. In *Against Heresies*, Book 5, Chapter 29, he wrote:

> And therefore, when in the end the Church shall be suddenly caught up from this, it is said, "There shall be Tribulation such as has not been since the beginning, neither shall be."[79]

In the above quote, Irenaeus used the same Greek word for "caught up," *harpazo*, that Paul used in 1 Thessalonians 4:17 for the Lord catching up living believers to meet Him in the air. Irenaeus placed this event ahead of a time of the "tribulation" Jesus referred to in Matthew 24:21. While this doesn't confirm that Irenaeus believed in a pre-Tribulation Rapture, it does reveal that he envisioned a fulfillment of the occurrence portrayed in 1 Thessalonians 4:17, the *harpazo*, followed by the time of extended Tribulation on the earth that Jesus talked about in Matthew 24:21ff. This also indicates that he regarded the Rapture and Second Coming as distinct and separate happenings.

The Shepherd of Hermas (about AD 140)

The Shepherd of Hermas is an allegory written about AD 140 that recounts several visions the Lord gave to a man named Hermas. In the fourth vision, Hermas encounters a great beast. He escapes the terror of the beast while at the same time he sees the Church appearing as "a virgin arrayed as if she were going forth from a bridal-chamber all in white and with white sandals, veiled up to her forehead, and her head-covering consisted of a turban, and her hair was white."

The virgin representing the Church then speaks these words to Hermas:

> Go therefore, and declare to the elect of the Lord his mighty works, and tell them that this beast is a type of the great tribulation which is to come. If therefore ye prepare yourselves beforehand, and repent (and turn) unto the Lord with your whole heart, ye shall be able to escape it, if your heart be made pure and without blemish, and if for the remaining days of your life ye serve the Lord blamelessly.[80]

The Shepherd of Hermas represents a second-century belief that the Church would escape a time of "great tribulation." The language fits with a belief in the pre-Tribulation Rapture. While we would not agree with the standard applied for inclusion of those who "escape" this time, it does signify a belief in what we now call the Rapture followed by a time of great Tribulation on the earth.

Cyprian (AD 200–258)

Cyprian, a bishop in the city of Carthage during the third century AD, guided his church through a time of intense persecution and suffering.

In his book, *Treatises of Cyprian,* he wrote:

> We who see that terrible things have begun, and know that still more terrible things are imminent, may regard it as the greatest advantage to depart from it as quickly as possible. Do you not give God thanks, do you not congratulate yourself, that by an early departure you are taken away, and delivered from the shipwrecks and disasters that are imminent? Let us greet the day which assigns each of us to his own home, which snatches us

> hence, and sets us free from the snares of the world and restores us to paradise and the kingdom.[81]

With these words, Cyprian expresses his belief in "an early departure" of the Church before further disasters occur on the earth. He believed the time of additional trouble was "imminent" and that a "departure" would take believers away so they wouldn't experience the troubling times ahead. His reference to "snatches us" sounds just like the catching up of the Church in 1 Thessalonians 4:17.

Notice the destination of those set "free from the snares of the world;" Jesus takes us to "paradise and the kingdom." According to Cyprian, we don't stay on earth; the Lord takes us to "paradise." This sounds remarkably similar to what many refer to today as pre-Tribulation Rapture, and again distinguishes it from Jesus' return to the earth.

The Apocalypse of Elijah (Third Century AD)

The *Apocalypse of Elijah* dates back to sometime in the third century AD. It's an apocryphal work that claims to be a revelation given by angels. The following quote is from author and teacher Dr. Francis Gumerlock's article in the October 2013 issue of *Bibliotheca Sacra*, the theological journal of Dallas Theological Seminary:

> According to chapter 3 of the Apocalypse of Elijah the "lawless one," that is, the Antichrist, will arrive on the world scene, will claim to be Christ, will set himself up in Jerusalem…Enoch & Elijah will return & oppose him…executing them…when the end-time persecution of the Antichrist intensifies, Christ will take pity on His people by sending Angels from heaven to snatch up those having the seal of God on their hands & foreheads… remove them from the wrath, and lead them to paradise. There

> raptured saints will receive white robes…& dwell in safety from Antichrist.… After this Christ will return with His saints, who reign with Him for a thousand years.[82]

In this excerpt, we see a distinction between the Rapture and the Second Coming. Jesus snatches up believers to "paradise" to remove them from "the wrath" on the earth during the Tribulation. After this time, the Church returns with Christ to "reign with Him for a thousand years."

The *Apocalypse of Elijah* confirms the presence of a belief similar to modern-day premillennialism as well as in a return of Jesus that is different than the Second Coming. It's more than a little significant that such beliefs existed within a couple centuries of when the apostles lived.

Ephraim the Syrian (AD 306–373)

An unmistakable reference to the pre-Tribulation Rapture comes from Saint Ephraim of Edessa, who was a monk, a poet, a writer of hymns, and a preacher during the fourth century.

The quote below comes from Ephraem's sermon entitled "On the Last Times, the Antichrist, and the End of the World." Some historians believe someone else wrote it in AD 622 and ascribed it to Ephraem in order to lend it credibility. Dr. Grant Jeffrey, who did extensive research on this sermon and obtained a translation of it on his own from a Greek scholar, believes it's more likely that Ephraem himself preached the sermon sometime around AD 323.[83]

> Believe you me, dearest brother, because the coming (advent) of the Lord is nigh, believe you me, because the end of the world is at hand, believe me, because it is the very last time. Or do you not believe unless you see with your eyes? See to it that this

> sentence be not fulfilled among you of the prophet who declares: "Woe to those who desire to see the day of the Lord!" For all the saints and elect of God are gathered, prior to the tribulation that is to come, and are taken to the Lord lest they see the confusion that is to overwhelm the world because of our sins.[84]

These words portray a belief in a pre-Tribulation Rapture dating back to the early fourth century AD. Even if we agree that someone wrote this sermon in AD 622 as some maintain, we still have a definitive reference to the pre-Tribulation Rapture in church history 1,200 years before John Darby lived. Notice the similarity between Ephraem's wording and that of 1 Thessalonians 5:9, which Paul wrote to confirm that believers will not see the wrath of the Day of the Lord. Ephraem warned against those who desired to "see the day of the Lord." He believed the promise that the Lord would deliver believers from this future time of furor.

Brother Dolcino (c. 1300)

In 1260, a man named Gerard Sagarello formed the Apostolic Brethren group in northern Italy. They encountered intense persecution from the Catholic Church since it was against the law to form any assembly separate from the Catholic Church.

A man referred to as Brother Dolcino later took over the leadership of the Apostolic Brethren, and it grew to several thousand in number. After Dolcino's death, an anonymous author in 1316 wrote *The History of Brother Dolcino*; below is a paragraph taken from it:

> Again, [Dolcino believed and preached and taught] that...the Antichrist was coming into this world within the bounds of the said three and a half years; and after he had come, then he

> [Dolcino] and his followers would be transferred into Paradise, in which are Enoch and Elijah. And in this way they will be preserved unharmed from the persecution of Antichrist. And that then Enoch and Elijah themselves would descend on the earth for the purpose of preaching [against] Antichrist. Then they would be killed by him or by his servants, and thus Antichrist would reign for a long time. But when the Antichrist is dead, Dolcino himself, who then would be the holy pope, and his preserved followers, will descend on the earth, and will preach the right faith of Christ to all, and will convert those who will be living then to the true faith of Jesus Christ.[85]

Though still heavily influenced by Roman Catholic theology, Dolcino nevertheless believed the Lord would transfer the Church into "paradise" to preserve believers "unharmed from the persecution of Antichrist." And while his view on the Second Coming is rather unique, to say the least, he does separate it from what we now refer to as the Rapture.

Morgan Edwards (1722–1795)

We have another clear reference to a pre-Tribulation Rapture before the time of John Darby; in this case, it's from a Welsh Baptist named Morgan Edwards.[86] Edwards wrote this about Jesus' appearing for His Church:

> I say, somewhat more—, because the dead saints will be raised, and the living changed at Christ's "appearing in the air" (I Thess. iv. 17); and this will be about three years and a half before the millennium, as we shall see hereafter: but will he and they abide in the air all that time? No: they will ascend to paradise, or to

some one of those many "mansions in the father's house" (John xiv. 2) and disappear during the foresaid period of time. The design of this retreat and disappearing will be to judge the risen and changed saints; for "now the time is come that judgment must begin," and that will be "at the house of God" (I Pet. iv. 17).[87]

Dr. Thomas Ice sums up the teaching of Edwards in this way:

Edwards makes three key points that are consistent with modern pretribulationism. First, he clearly separates the rapture from the second coming by an interval of three and-a-half years. Second, he uses modern pre-trib rapture verses (1 Thessalonians 4:17 and John 14:2) to describe the rapture and support his view. Third, he believed the judgment seat of Christ (rewarding) for believers will occur in heaven while the tribulation is raging on earth, as is common in contemporary pretribulationism.[88]

Other quotes from Edwards confirm that he believed in a three-and half-year Tribulation just as did John Darby at first, before he came to the conviction that it would last seven years. This doesn't diminish the presence of a belief that the Rapture would occur before a time of Tribulation a century before the time of John Darby.

Summing Up

The belief in Jesus' return for believers before a time of catastrophic troubles on the earth existed well before the nineteenth century. There's evidence of such convictions as early as the second and third centuries. In addition, many through the years have regarded Rapture as a distinct and separate event from the Second Coming.

History doesn't prove or disprove any doctrine; Scripture alone must be our sole source of belief and practice. The evidence, however, refutes the belief in a catching-up of the saints prior to a time of Tribulation on the earth did not begin until relatively late in church history.

Furthermore, John Darby alone cannot account for why the belief in a pre-Tribulation Rapture grew to the point that it dominated the evangelical church in America as well as in many other countries for much of the twentieth century.

This widespread appeal of belief in the pre-Tribulation Rapture happened because pastors, writers, and teachers correctly expounded the many texts that teach the appearing of Jesus for His Church before the start of the Tribulation.

Adherence to the pre-Tribulation Rapture came about as the next logical step after premillennialism that gradually took hold throughout the church after the Reformation. As teachers and scholars rejected the pagan allegorical interpretations of Scripture and anti-Semitism that sadly characterized the church of the Dark Ages, the emphasis shifted to treating prophetic passages in the way that the biblical authors intended them. As a result, belief in the Rapture occurring before the Tribulation flourished in Bible-believing churches across the world for almost a century before the return to allegorical interpretations of biblical prophecy once again took hold in many places.

20

The Biblical Necessity of the Pre-Tribulation Rapture

> Pretribulationism is the only view that makes "the blessed hope" (Titus 2:13) truly a blessed hope. Few doctrines have brought more hope to grieving and persecuted souls during the past 2000 years than the doctrine of the blessed hope, which is the teaching that Christ will return for His church, resurrect the dead, and transport living believers to be with Himself while the world endures the Tribulation.
>
> -Tim LaHaye, *The Popular Encyclopedia of Bible Prophecy*[89]

Despite the growing dissension within the church regarding the Rapture, I remain convinced that Jesus is coming for all His saints, for us, before the start of the Tribulation. This isn't something I could have written with such confidence ten or perhaps even five years ago.

Since my seminary training and decades of study in this area turned into a full-time writing ministry in 2016, I've become even more persuaded of the sound biblical foundation for the pre-Tribulation Rapture. This happened as I continued to study biblical texts regarding the Rapture and then put my thoughts regarding these passages into words, as I've done in the preceding chapters.

My main purpose in writing about the Rapture is to encourage believers to remain watchful as signs of the approaching Tribulation abound all around us. Despite the many disappointments we endure in this life, we can know with certainty that Jesus is coming for us before the Tribulation, the extended time of God's wrath upon the Christ-rejecting world.

My intent for this chapter is to summarize the preceding chapters as well as show how each assertion builds on the one before it.

1. Premillennialism Is a Biblical Certainty

In any quest to establish the biblical soundness of the pre-Tribulation Rapture, we must absolutely begin with this question: Is premillennialism biblical? If we deny the reality of a seven-year Tribulation, then it makes no difference where we place the Rapture, since there are no future devastating judgments for us to avoid.

In addition, those who say there is no future Tribulation and deny the thousand-year reign of Jesus do so through the use of allegory rather than on the original intent of the authors of Scripture.

Of course, the biblical writers do employ symbolism at times. That's far, far different, however, than imposing an allegorical paradigm on biblical texts where the author is communicating objective thoughts regarding the future of Israel and of the earth.

We thus start with assumptions that premillennialism is true and that we must interpret biblical prophecy according to the intent of the author. All my arguments in favor of a pre-Tribulation rapture rest on these two foundations.

2. The Rapture Cannot Happen at the Same Time as the Second Coming

Proceeding on the basis that premillennialism is a biblical necessity, we come to another matter in our quest to establish the biblical necessity of the pre-Tribulation Rapture: Is it the same even as the Second Coming?

If it is, this would place the Lord's appearing for us at the conclusion of the seven years of Tribulation and thus end our pursuit (some premillennialists also combine the two).

However, the biblical texts that describe the Rapture and Second Coming differ significantly in many ways that render it impossible to reconcile the two events into one.

The timing of the resurrection of those who have died in Christ confirms this distinction. The resurrection of the dead happens first in the order of events that Paul describes in 1 Thessalonians 4:13–17 and in 1 Corinthians 15:50–54. In the Second Coming, the resurrection of Tribulation saints does not happen until after a lengthy sequence of many other events (see Revelation 19:11–20:4); it may not even occur until several days after Jesus begins His return to the earth.

Please also note that the resurrection of the dead in Revelation 20:4 includes only a subset of believers, the Tribulation saints, while the passages referring to the Rapture emphasize that Jesus raises *all* the dead in Christ. This not only distinguishes the two events, but necessitates a significant time lapse between them for people to come to Christ and experience martyrdom.

These are just two of several substantial differences between biblical passages describing the Rapture versus those referring to the Second Coming. *If the words of Scripture matter, and they do, then we cannot combine these two events into one occurrence.*

See chapter 10 for additional variances between the Rapture and Second Coming.

3. The New Testament Expectation of Jesus' Appearing

The sense of imminence in the New Testament regarding Jesus' appearing further establishes the Rapture as a distinct event and pushes it to a time before the events of the Tribulation commence. The apostles repeatedly described their readers as eagerly anticipating Jesus' return for them (1 Corinthians 1:7; Philippians 3:20–21; 1 Thessalonians 1:8–10;

Titus 2:11–13; James 5:8; 1 Peter 1:13). New Testament saints watched for the Rapture as though it could occur at any moment.

As for the Second Coming, Jesus told us that at least two major events would happen before it. In Matthew 24:15–29, He says that the defilement of the Temple by the Antichrist and the "great tribulation" that follows it will happen before He returns to earth. *According to the Lord's own words, significant events that have not yet happened must occur before the Second Coming. This cannot happen today or tomorrow because so much has to take place before the Lord can return to the earth.*

Do you see how the expectation of the Second Coming thus differs from that of the New Testament saints who prayed for Jesus to return soon (*maranatha*)? In his early letters, Paul expressed the anticipation that he might be alive at the time of Jesus' appearing. This is only possible with a pre-Tribulation Rapture.

This sense of imminence not only confirms that a significant amount of time passes between the Rapture and Second Coming, but also seemingly places it ahead of the events that the Bible says will occur during the Tribulation.

4. A New Testament Example of the Imminent Expectation of the Rapture

Having examined the excited anticipation of Jesus' imminent appearing that Paul wrote about in Philippians 3:20–21, we might ask: "Does the New Testament provide an example of such an expectation?"

Yes, it does. A close look at 1 Thessalonians 4:13–18 reveals the recipients of Paul's letter not only believed that the Rapture *could* happen in their lifetime, but mistakenly assumed that it *would* happen before they died.

We see this in the way that Paul addresses the unnecessary grieving of the new converts in Thessalonica over the deaths of some in their midst.

If their sorrow had stemmed from a lack of belief in the future resurrection of their loved ones, Paul would have responded in the same way that he addressed this issue with those in Corinth (see 1 Corinthians chapter 15), but he doesn't do that. Instead, he attributes their grief to a lack of information rather than a lack of faith in the promise of a future resurrection. In response, the apostle gives them further revelation regarding the Rapture, emphasizing the role of the "dead in Christ" during Jesus' appearing (1 Thessalonians 4:13–16).

Paul's emphasis in these verses reveals the source of the problem: The Thessalonians mistakenly thought that the dead in Christ would miss out on the joy of the Rapture. So, in response to their grief, the apostle stresses the prominent role of the dead in Christ during Jesus' appearing (4:13–16). Why would he reply in such a way if this were not the cause of their unnecessary mourning?

5. The Surprise Beginning of the Day of the Lord

For me, the differences between the Rapture and Second Coming, along with the sense of imminence, confirm that Jesus' appearing will happen before the start of the Tribulation, but this isn't the case with many other believers. I remember hearing a sermon during which the preacher combined the Rapture and Second Coming, but then at the end of his message, he told us that the Lord could return that very afternoon. How is that possible?

I've discovered that many who say Jesus' return is imminent also teach that it will happen during the Tribulation, at its end, or at the end of the age. Such thinking necessitates that we dig deeper in order to establish that our anticipation of Jesus' soon appearing signifies that we will miss *all* of the Rapture.

In 1 Thessalonians 5:2–3, Paul tells his readers that the start of the Day of the Lord will surprise people on the earth "like a thief in the night" with its "sudden destruction" from which "they will not escape."

The Day of Lord, a primarily Old Testament term, refers to an extended time of the Lord's wrath on the earth leading up to and including Jesus' return.

If the Day of the Lord began at any time after the seal judgments of Revelation 6 commence, this day wouldn't catch anyone by surprise. No one will be saying "peace and security" (v. 3) after the pestilences, famines, pandemics, and wars of the seal judgments kill one-fourth of the earth's population.

In 1 Thessalonians 5:9, the apostle assures his readers, and us, that we will not experience this time of God's judgment upon the earth: "For God has not destined us for wrath, but to obtain salvation through our Lord Jesus Christ." Since the seal judgments are a part of God's wrath, the Lord must come for us before they begin.

6. The Panic of the Thessalonians Confirms That They Expected to Miss the Tribulation

Thanks to some troublemakers who told the saints in Thessalonica that the Day of the Lord had already begun, we know that these new converts expected the Rapture to happen before the start of the Day of the Lord and thus before the beginning of the Tribulation.

In 2 Thessalonians 2:2, Paul responds to this errant message by telling his readers "not to be quickly shaken in mind or alarmed, either by a spirit or a spoken word, or a letter seeming to be from us, to the effect that the day of the Lord has come." The words imply that the Thessalonians literally trembled with fear when they heard that this day had already begun.

Why would they panic at such news if they expected to be on earth during the day of the Lord—or even for a part of it? Their response to the false report tells us they regarded Paul's promise in 1 Thessalonians 5:9 as one of deliverance from all of God's wrath during the day of the Lord, which includes all of the seven-year Tribulation. See chapter 14 for much more on how the fear of the Thessalonian saints confirms that they expected the Rapture to occur before the Tribulation.

7. The Departure of 2 Thessalonians 2:3 Denotes a Pre-Tribulation Rapture

In 2 Thessalonians 2:3 Paul wrote:

> Let no one deceive you in any way. For that day will not come, unless the rebellion comes first, and the man of lawlessness is revealed, the son of destruction.

The Greek word *apostasia,* often translated "rebellion," literally means "departure." The context alone determines whether this word refers to a physical parting, such as the Rapture, or a spiritual apostasy, which is a common understanding for 2 Thessalonians 2:3.

Both the immediate context of the verse as well as of the two letters Paul wrote to the Thessalonians support the idea of a physical departure over that of leaving the faith. The definite article in the Greek tells us that the apostle has a definite event in mind, one the Thessalonians would recognize without further explanation. We have no evidence that Paul talked to the Thessalonians about a future apostasy. He didn't write about the church's departure from the faith in the last days until much later in his ministry.

On the other hand, both his letters to the Thessalonians refer directly to the Rapture in almost every chapter; that's a departure they would have readily recognized apart from Paul offering a word of clarification as to what *apostasia* meant.

If the departure of 2 Thessalonians 2:3 denotes the Rapture, and the evidence strongly points to that conclusion, then that event *must* happen before the start of the Tribulation.

8. The Unveiling of the Antichrist to the World

In Paul's response to the panic of the Thessalonians saints concerning the perceived start to the Day of the Lord, he tells them they can know that this day has not yet begun because the Restrainer continues to hold back the unveiling of the Antichrist (2 Thessalonians 2:3–8). In other words, Satan cannot reveal his "man of lawlessness" to the world while they remain earthbound.

If the Restrainer is the Holy Spirit, and no other interpretation fits better with these verses, this also confirms that the Church cannot be on earth when the Antichrist steps to the forefront of the world's stage. According to what Paul writes in 2 Thessalonians 2:3–8, the Restrainer will hold back the "man of lawlessness" until this unique ministry concludes with the Rapture.

The identification of the Holy Spirit as the Restrainer signifies that the unveiling of the Antichrist to the world cannot occur before the Rapture.

9. Jesus' Promise to the Church at Philadelphia

If a pre-Tribulation Rapture is a sound biblical teaching, we would expect to find support for it in the book of Revelation, and that is exactly what we see.

In Revelation 3:10, Jesus said:

> Because you have kept my word about patient endurance, I will keep you from the hour of trial that is coming on the whole world, to try those who dwell on the earth.

This "hour of trial" doesn't refer to a time of persecution that would come upon that particular church; rather, it speaks of a time of suffering that will impact *all* the people of the world, which fits with the Tribulation John describes in Revelation 6–18.

Jesus' words that immediately follow tell us how He will keep us out of the "hour of trial" that will fall upon the world: "I am coming quickly" (Revelation 3:11). We know that Jesus did not return in any way during the lifetime of this church. This helps us understand that the promise applies to believers today. As we examined in chapter 17, both "the hour of trial" and the designation of "those who dwell on the earth" fit perfectly with what the Apostle John wrote about in Revelation 6–18.

10. The Church Is in Heaven Before the Tribulation Starts

If the Church isn't on earth during the Tribulation or the "hour of trial," it must be in heaven with Jesus. The appearance of the twenty-four elders seated on thrones in heaven confirms that the Church in fact will be in heaven with Jesus before the Tribulation on earth (Revelation 4–5). John's portrayal of these people fits with promises made to New Testament saints, and not to angels. The term "elder" denotes an aging process, which means they are not angels.

If these elders represent the Church, and no other possibility fits John's depiction of them, this places all New Testament saints in heaven before the seal judgments of Revelation 6.

11. The Need for Witnesses During the Tribulation

If the Church remains on the earth during the Tribulation, why is there a need for other witnesses to the saving message of the gospel? As discussed earlier, in a radio interview with Jan Markell on November 7, 2020, Amir Tsarfati questioned the need for the two witnesses of Revelation 11:1–13 if the Church is present on earth at the start of the Tribulation. Isn't it the job of the Church to bear witness of the gospel during this current age?

However, in Revelation 14:6–7, John writes:

> Then I saw another angel flying directly overhead, with an eternal gospel to proclaim to those who dwell on earth, to every

> nation and tribe and language and people. And he said with a loud voice, "Fear God and give him glory, because the hour of his judgment has come, and worship him who made heaven and earth, the sea and the springs of water."

Why does the Lord need to send an angel to proclaim the gospel to the people of the earth if the Church is still present? This only makes sense with a pre-Tribulation Rapture and the absence of the Church during this period. Otherwise, it would be the task of believers to keep fulfilling the Great Commission.

Amir also brought up the 144,000 Jews that God will seal during the Tribulation (Revelation 7:1–8), whom many believe will act as evangelists during that time. If the Church remains on earth during this time, why does the Lord need to give these Israelites special protection so that they may evangelize the world? And if the Rapture has not yet occurred, what makes these select Hebrews different than other members of the Body of Christ of which Paul says that both "Greek and Jew" maintain identical footing in Him (Colossians 3:11)?

12. Galilean Wedding Traditions

Not only do the Jewish wedding customs of the first century AD help us understand the joy of Jesus' return for us, but they picture a pre-Tribulation Rapture. After the betrothal ceremony, the groom leaves to prepare a place for the couple in his father's home. When his father determines that he's finished his task, he sends the groom to fetch his bride.

We see these identical elements in both Jesus' words in the upper room and in Paul's description of the Rapture in 1 Thessalonians. The disciples, who were all Galilean, could not have missed the similarities between Jesus' appearing and the wedding traditions they had observed in their hometowns. The picture is of Jesus coming for us before a time of great wrath upon the earth.[90] It illustrates a pre-Tribulation Rapture.

God Has Not Destined Us for Wrath

Jesus is coming for His followers before the start of the Day of the Lord; that is the promise of 1 Thessalonians 5:9:

> For God has not destined us for wrath, but to obtain salvation through our Lord Jesus Christ.

The church cannot be on the earth during the seal judgments that result in the deaths of a fourth of the world's population. This is the wrath the Lord, through the Apostle Paul, promises us we will miss.

When Jesus appears, He will take all those who belong to Him back to the place He's preparing for us. (See the appendix for why I believe that Jesus will not leave any born-again saint behind when He comes for His Church.)

Section Four

The Triumph of the Redeemed

Why have I put so much effort into establishing the biblical truths of premillennialism and the pre-Tribulation Rapture? It's because these teachings not only honor the intent of the *words* of Scripture, but they alone provide the specifics of our hope that result in a gospel-driven, two-world perspective, one that mimics that of the Apostle Paul (see 2 Corinthians 4:17–18; Romans 8:18). These truths confirm the splendor of the future triumph we will someday share because of our union with Jesus Christ.

They are the reason we can consider ourselves "more than conquerors" (Romans 8:37) when our circumstances tell a much, much different story. Our future does not depend upon better circumstances or on improving conditions on earth, but in God's steadfast love for us that shows itself in the amazing future He has planned for us.

I believe the Lord revealed many of the specifics of our life eternity in order to encourage us *each day* as we step out of bed knowing just how difficult and painful life is.

Although many who advocate various forms of amillennialism would beg to differ with my assessment regarding the necessity of premillennialism for a hopeful, two-world outlook on life, their signless, end-of-the-age wrap-up of human history doesn't typically awaken joyous thoughts of eternity in anyone, nor does it lift believers above solely earthbound perspectives on life.

Because amillennialists either ignore or distort passages such as 1 Corinthians 15:51–57, 1 Thessalonians 4:13–18, and Philippians 3:20–21, they rarely, if ever, talk about the immortal bodies that Jesus will give us at His appearing. I came away from one such presentation of the Second Coming wondering if existing under such a view of eternity would be that much different than what we experience now. The lack of reference to our imperishable bodies and the denial of a literal New Jerusalem made eternity seem lifeless and uninspiring to me. What was there to forward to?

Do you see how this differs from our exciting expectation of Jesus' appearing, our immortality, a celebration in heaven, our return with Him, our reign with Him during the Millennium, and our enjoyment of eternity as described in the words of Revelation 21–22? *The premillennial view of future events and circumstances is exponentially more exciting than anything we could dream up on our own.*

The joyful events described in this section comprise the future tense of the gospel. They remind us each day that a much better life awaits, one that's full of joy, health, immortality, restoration, wonder, unending adventures, and unimaginable beauty.

In Jesus, we are more than conquerors, regardless of what life throws at us or the depressing news reports that come our way each day. Nothing here below can separate us from His love (Romans 8:31–38). So stayed tuned as we explore a few of the things promised to us as part of our eternal inheritance.

21

We Will Receive Immortal Bodies

> Inside your body, even if it is failing, is the blueprint for your resurrection body. You may not be satisfied with your current body or mind—but you'll be thrilled with your resurrection upgrades. With them you'll be better able to serve and glorify God and enjoy an eternity of wonders he has prepared for you.
>
> -Randy Alcorn, *Heaven*[91]

Our future triumph in Christ begins with the Rapture; that's when the Lord will transform "our lowly body to be like his glorious body" (Philippians 3:20–21) and catch us up to be with Him in the clouds (1 Thessalonians 4:17). Although we discussed this outcome of our faith in the chapters dealing with the Rapture, it also belongs in the discussion of our future triumph in Christ. It's the mainstay of our imminent expectation and one we cannot overemphasize in these last days.

The brief and fleeting allusions to eternal life after death we so often hear today rarely resonate with those in the pews. Pastors and teachers who ignore our hope more often than not make death rather than our departure to paradise the expectation of the saints. They might refer to Jesus' imminent return, but then deny its possibility by pushing the timing of it to the end of the age, which everyone assumes is in the far-distant future.

I remember hearing one preacher loudly proclaiming that everyone in attendance would someday die. Not only does such a statement contradict what Paul stated in 1 Thessalonians 4:17 and 1 Corinthians 15:51–52, but for me it put a definite damper on that Resurrection Sunday service.

I'm not saying that everyone reading this book will live until the Rapture (although I believe it's exceedingly close), but the Bible teaches us to live in anticipation of that spectacular day when Jesus gives us a glorious, imperishable body, grants us an inner wholeness that we can only dream about in this life, and completes our adoption into God's family so that it becomes our joyous experience rather than just a reality of our faith.

The "blessed hope" of Titus 2:13 was a key part of the proclamation of the gospel in the early days of the church. How else can one explain the depth of the Thessalonians; knowledge about Jesus' return for them, the arrival of the Antichrist, and the Day of the Lord after Paul's very brief stay in the city that may have been little more than a month?

An Immortal New Body

When Jesus comes to take us home to heaven, we will receive immortal and imperishable bodies. Doesn't this lift our eyes upward during the many difficulties of life? Paul assured the saints in Philippi of this stunning expectation:

> But our citizenship is in heaven, and from it we await a Savior, the Lord Jesus Christ, who will transform our lowly body to be

> like his glorious body, by the power that enables him even to subject all things to himself. (Philippians 3:20–21).

The apostle says our future bodies will be just like Jesus' after He rose from the dead.

In 1 Corinthians 15:52b–53, the Lord reveals more details of this:

> For the trumpet will sound, and the dead will be raised imperishable, and we shall be changed. For this perishable body must put on the imperishable, and this mortal body must put on immortality.

We will receive immortal physical bodies the moment Jesus returns for us (aka the Rapture).

If we are alive at the time of His appearing, Jesus will instantly transform our aging and achy forms into immortal and imperishable ones. If we die before the Rapture, this is the time He will bring our dead bodies to life again and join them with our souls that are already with Him (1 Thessalonians 4:13–17).

This exchange of our dying or dead bodies for eternal, resurrected ones will be like swapping an old rusted out Ford Pinto, perhaps held together with duct tape, for a brand-new, shiny red Porsche Carrera, or perhaps a black Rolls-Royce. However, our new bodies will never deteriorate, grow old, or wear out as even the best-built and most expensive cars will do over time.

Our new bodies will forever remain immune to all sicknesses, pandemics, cancer, and any other disease you can name! This means the end of all doctor and dentist appointments (and chiropractors, too). No more vaccinations and shots! We will forget about our aches, pains, physical suffering, and the effects of aging; we'll someday regard these maladies as relics of our distant past.

What an amazing expectation! Doesn't this sure promise of an immortal and imperishable body brighten your day as you watch for Jesus' appearing? It does mine.

Inner Wholeness

In his book *All Things New*, John Eldredge says:

> We are all traumatized and fragmented; no one passes through this vale of tears without it. And our Healer will make us whole again.... Think of it—to be wholehearted. To be filled with goodness from head to toe. To have an inner glory that matches the glory of your new body...[92]

In the opening chapters of this book, I shared my story of how the Lord healed the deep wounds of my past that had caused my PTSD. Although I've experienced Jesus' wonderful and dramatic healing since that time, I still yearn for the total inner wholeness about which John Eldredge writes. I continue to feel "traumatized and fragmented" at times. The scars from my past, however, serve as ever-present reminders that a much, much better day lies ahead.

I'm grateful for all the storms that the Lord has allowed into my life and how they have all prepared me for my current ministry of writing as well as for my role in eternity. The brokenness and weakness I feel remind me that this moment is not all I have.

My soul longs for the increased sharpness of mind, completed emotional healing, and Jesus' total deliverance from the presence of sin that will someday be mine along with my transformed body. Isn't this part of the groaning the Apostle Paul referred to in 2 Corinthians 5:4–5? I think so; I call it "sanctified groaning."

Can you understand why I so vigorously defend premillennialism and the pre-Tribulation Rapture? First, for me, it's not just a matter of being doctrinally sound, but of defending what I wholeheartedly believe Scripture teaches. Second, prophecy confirms that God remains in control over history as the days grower darker and increasingly violent. That not only keeps my heart at peace, but assures me that God will judge the wickedness we see everywhere and will someday establish His Son, Jesus, as King to rule over the nations. In contrast to the widespread corruption and deceit inherent in so many governments, the Lord will reign in total righteousness.

These aren't meaningless beliefs without relevance to our daily lives as we deal with financial woes, betrayals by those we once trusted, shattered dreams, and growing anxieties over increased violence and lawlessness in our world. These pillars of our gospel hope enable us to look beyond "this vale of tears" to our glorious future where we will live forever in immortal bodies that are free from the presence of sin and all the handicaps that pile upon us as we journey through this life.

The promise of Jesus' soon appearing empowers us to endure frightful days and sleepless, tear-filled nights because of our certain hope of a coming day in which we will share in Jesus' triumph over death and forever reign with Him.

Dying side by side with the Christ-rejecting earth-dwellers as they experience the outpouring of God's wrath on this world is most assuredly NOT the "blessed hope" of Titus 2:11–14, nor is it the encouragement of 1 Thessalonians 4:18 and 5:11.

No, no, no! Our expectation consists of seeing Jesus face to face at any moment, and that moment looms ever so close as we now watch the Tribulation come at us like an out-of-control freight train.

The Rapture is the joyous gospel anticipation that Paul proclaimed everywhere in the ancient world; that's when our lowly bodies become like His. This, however, only begins our incredible adventure of sharing Jesus' triumph over sin and death.

22

We Will Celebrate with Great Jubilation

Then I heard again what sounded like the shout of a vast crowd or the roar of mighty ocean waves or the crash of loud thunder:

> "Praise the Lord! For the Lord our God, the Almighty, reigns. Let us be glad and rejoice, and let us give honor to him. For the time has come for the wedding feast of the Lamb and his bride has prepared herself. She has been given the finest of pure white linen to wear." For the fine linen represents the good deeds of God's holy people.
>
> ~Revelation 19:6–8, New Living Translation

The noise suddenly became deafening. Before that point in the game, the Iowa crowd was quiet and subdued as it looked like Indiana was about to score another touchdown and seal their apparent victory. The mood in the stadium suddenly changed when the Indiana quarterback lost control of the football and an Iowa player, Tyler Sash, grabbed the loose ball off the back of another player and ran it back eighty-six yards for a touchdown. By the time he reached the goal line, all seventy thousand Iowa fans were standing and cheering ecstatically.

The scene described in Revelation 19:1–8 reminds me of the excitement I felt that day in the stands as Sash raced toward the end zone, but on a much grander scale. The shouts of joy during this future time will emanate from a much greater multitude of people who will all be praising God with all their heart and soul.

As members of the Bride of Christ, we will join in this great jubilation of thunderous acclaim for our Lord and Savior. This is yet another aspect of how we will someday take part in Jesus' triumph.

The Occasion for the Jubilation

Revelation 18 provides the reason for the thunderously loud praise of chapter 19: the defeat of Babylon. Many differing interpretations exist as to what "Babylon" represents in this context. For the purposes of this chapter, I will assume it signifies, in some form, Satan's earthly realm over which Antichrist rules during the Tribulation. At the height of Antichrist's rule over the nations of the world, he will kill a multitude of people who refuse to take his mark for buying and selling goods (Revelation 13:15–18).

I believe we see this coming global government—or at the very least, a precursor to it—in the New World Order or what the World Economic Forum fondly refers to as the "Great Reset." The intent of globalists is no longer a secret; they openly discuss their intent to use the COVID-19 panic, as well as climate alarm, to gain increased control over the world's population. Their Marxist-driven agenda will at some point enslave all peoples of the world, just as the Bible says will happen during the coming Tribulation.

Revelation 18 records the demise of Antichrist's reign of terror, which also signals the impending destruction of him and the False Prophet at Jesus' return (Revelation 19:20). *It's after the defeat of Satan's wicked and deadly earthly kingdom that ear-deafening rejoicing and praise breaks out in heaven, and understandably so.*

Participants in the Great Jubilation

Revelation 19:1–5 also identifies the members of this "great multitude in heaven" who fill heaven with jubilant praise at the downfall of Babylon.

The first group John mentions are the Tribulation saints, those killed by the Antichrist during his reign of terror (19:2). We see this group in Revelation 6:9–11 crying out to God to avenge their blood, which the Lord does at the end of the Tribulation as He destroys Babylon, the kingdom that brought about their martyrdom.

Revelation 19:4 identifies a second assembly of worshipers expressing adoration for the Lord as the "twenty-four elders." In chapter 17, I explain why this group must represent the Church in heaven during the time of Tribulation on earth. They cannot be angels, because the Bible never pictures them as sitting on thrones or possessing crowns, as do these elders (Revelation 4:4).

One more group of voices, along with those of the Tribulation saints and the angelic host, will fill heaven with loud hallelujahs as we celebrate the fatal blows to the kingdom of the Antichrist: ours. What a wonderful day it will be! Can you imagine the excitement we will feel at this time?

The Lord God Omnipotent Reigns

Revelation 19:6 records another reason for our raucous praise that will someday resound through heavens like "the roar of many waters...and the sound of mighty peals of thunder." It's the announcement that Jesus rules over the nations, which John describes in Revelation 20:4–10.

I like the King James Version translation of the end of verse 6 as reflected in the "Hallelujah Chorus" from "Messiah": "for the Lord God omnipotent reigneth." Regardless of whether we will someday sing this specific joyous and goosebump-causing chorus composed by Handel, we will experience firsthand the exuberant anticipation of Jesus' coming rule expressed by this song. If not the "Hallelujah Chorus," I believe we will sing something even more majestic and thrilling at some point during Jesus' ascension to the throne of David.

Our celebration will also include the Marriage Supper of the Lamb, as described in Revelation 19:7–9. Some say this happens *after* the Second Coming, which John describes in the rest of this chapter. I favor placing the timing of this feast *before* we return with Jesus to reign with Him during Millennium.

Why Does This Matter for Us Today?

As we take part in the jubilance described Revelation 19:1–8, we will likely remember what we saw of Satan's evil kingdom before the Rapture: barbaric abortions, the murder of infants who survive abortions, abhorrent sex trafficking, the redefining of marriage, the killing of believers around the world, rampant pedophilia, the insidious promotion of transgenderism, and the many displays of lawlessness and violence that seemingly multiply by the day.

Scripture doesn't specify whether we will see the events of the Tribulation after Jesus takes us to paradise. Since Revelation 19 indicates that we'll be aware of the Lord's destruction of Satan's future kingdom, what many now refer to as the Great Reset, perhaps we'll witness it from our lofty vantage point. Since the Tribulation saints will celebrate with us, we'll likely hear their accounts of the terror on the earth from them.

The destruction of Babylon (Revelation 18) signifies that the Lord will have the final word on all the widespread evil so evident in our world. We most likely will never see the perpetrators of evil and injustice go to jail, but we can know with absolute certainty that a day of reckoning is coming for all those who persist in rejecting the Savior's offer of eternal life.

Yes, we will celebrate once the kingdom of the Antichrist lies in ruins, for that signifies that the reign of our righteous King and Savior is about to encompass the world.

23

We Will Take Part in Jesus' Glorious Return

> The second coming of Christ will be so revolutionary that it will change every aspect of life on this planet. Christ will reign in righteousness. Disease will be arrested. Death will be modified. War will be abolished. Nature will be changed. Man will live as it was originally intended he should live.
>
> ~Billy Graham, *Billy Graham in Quotes*

In late 1971, the song "Imagine," written and performed by the late John Lennon, started its climb to the top of the charts. Its words encourage "the listener to imagine a world at peace without the barriers of borders or the divisions of religion and nationality, and to consider the possibility that the focus of humanity should be living a life unattached to material possessions."[93] The lyrics envision a united world without borders, a new world order apart from any recognition of God.

The song espouses an atheistic and humanistic viewpoint that asks the listener to deny the reality of heaven and hell and thereby any consequence for one's behavior, good or otherwise. It's a world devoid of faith in the Lord, which is what the current advocates of the Great Reset envision for our world.

Can such a reorganization of the world begin an era of peace on the planet?

The evidence says "No!" The elimination of God from the public square has already resulted in much less harmony to the world, which will only get much worse until the time Jesus returns to set up His kingdom. The socialistic type of government envisioned by Lennon has resulted in a great loss of life during the past century, and will surely do so again in the future.

The dream of everyone on the planet living as a united humanity remains the goal of many today, but with no viable hope of realization due in large part to the fallenness of human nature. In addition, the utopia offered by the globalists is a deceitful play to lure people into accepting their agenda. The end will be far different than the one that the elite present to people.

However, Scripture reveals a much better future that begins with the Second Coming.

Imagine Jesus' Triumphant Return to Earth

Imagine along with me a much different scenario than the one John Lennon envisioned, one in which a powerful King leads a force of millions upon millions of His followers into war. This King, appearing majestically upon a white horse, does not approach the battle from the land or sea, or even from the air in a traditional sense, but He magnificently rides across the sky with His vast army behind Him, also riding on white horses.

Imagine people from every nation watching the return of this glorious and all-powerful King.

Jesus' Second Coming will be the most spectacular event that anyone will ever see. He will come with overwhelming might and bright shining glory beyond anything we can now envision. At His First Coming, Christ arrived as a baby in a manger, which denoted the lowliest of circumstances. The contrast with His future return to earth could not be any greater.

Jesus' return will forever change life in this world and usher in an era of peace beyond anything John Lennon could have envisioned. Religion will no longer exist; that's true. *Everyone on the planet will worship Jesus, at least at first.*

The prophet Habakkuk referred to the impact of Jesus' Second Coming with these words:

> For the earth will be filled with the knowledge of the glory of the Lord as the waters cover the sea. (Habakkuk 2:14)

At the start of Jesus' millennial kingdom, all the people of the earth will know and love the Lord. The world will experience a righteous harmony based on Jesus, not the godless and lifeless unity about which Lennon sang.

John's Vision of Jesus' Return

I love the Apostle John's description of Jesus as He prepares to return to earth. In Revelation 19:11–16, we read:

> Then I saw heaven opened, and behold, a white horse! The one sitting on it is called Faithful and True, and in righteousness he judges and makes war. His eyes are like a flame of fire, and on his head are many diadems, and he has a name written that no one knows but himself. He is clothed in a robe dipped in blood, and the name by which he is called is The Word of God. And the armies of heaven, arrayed in fine linen, white and pure, were following him on white horses. From his mouth comes a sharp sword with which to strike down the nations, and he will rule

> them with a rod of iron. He will tread the winepress of the fury of the wrath of God the Almighty. On his robe and on his thigh he has a name written, King of kings and Lord of lords.

In these verses, John emphasizes the power, splendor, and radiance of our Lord as "King of kings." He focuses our attention on Jesus' eternal greatness, His deity, and His total victory over all the powers of darkness. Christ will return with majesty never seen on the earth and power beyond anything we have seen.

As redeemed saints, we will share in Jesus' triumphant return to earth. We will ride on the white horses behind Him as He rides back to take control of the nations.

In Revelation 1:7, John describes the Lord's return:

> Behold, he is coming with the clouds, and every eye will see him, even those who pierced him, and all tribes of the earth will wail on account of him.

Jesus' return to earth will not be a hidden event or even one that a few will witness; everyone on earth will see it.

Jesus Described His Return

Jesus' own description of His return to earth fits well with the words describing it in the book of Revelation. In Matthew 24:29–31 we read:

> Immediately after the tribulation of those days the sun will be darkened, and the moon will not give its light, and the stars will fall from heaven, and the powers of the heavens will be shaken. Then will appear in heaven the sign of the Son of Man, and then all the tribes of the earth will mourn, and they will see the Son

> of Man coming on the clouds of heaven with power and great glory. And he will send out his angels with a loud trumpet call, and they will gather his elect from the four winds, from one end of heaven to the other.

This event will be a worldwide sensation! After He defeats His enemies and takes control of the world, Jesus will send out His angels to "gather his elect" from all areas of the earth. The angels will bring them to a location, presumably near Jerusalem, where the faithful and the "elect" Israelis who survive the Tribulation will enter the Millennium in their natural bodies.

Jesus referred to His prophesied return while on trial before Caiaphas, the high priest, and the Sanhedrin. The high priest demanded that Jesus admit His identity as "the Christ, the Son of God" (Matthew 26:63). Caiaphas, of course, had no interest in worshiping Him, but was seeking a blasphemous claim he could use to convict Him.

Jesus responded:

> You have said so. But I tell you, from now on you will see the Son of Man seated at the right hand of Power and coming on the clouds of heaven. (v. 64)

With these words, Jesus told the high priest that He would fulfill the words of Daniel 7:13–14. In doing so, He claimed to be the "Son of Man" whom Daniel prophesied would destroy kingdoms of the world and establish an everlasting dominion.

Scriptural References to Jesus' Second Coming

Both the New and Old Testaments tell us about the return of the Messiah to the nation of Israel. Daniel 7, the passage Jesus referenced in His reply, is just one of many passages that look forward to the Second Coming. Dr. Grant R. Jeffrey made this comment regarding the number of references to Jesus' return in both testaments:

> The Second Coming of Jesus Christ is the greatest single theme in Scripture. While there are approximately three hundred prophecies in the Old Testament that foretold the first coming of Christ, there are more than eight times as many verses describing the Second Coming. In total, some 2400 verses throughout the Old and New Testaments reveal God's promises about the return of Jesus Christ. The enormous number of prophetic verses about the Second Coming underlines the vital importance of this event in God's plan for mankind.[94]

The Old Testament prophets spoke often and repeatedly of the Second Coming. Zechariah chapters 12 and 14, for example, tell us about the defeat of the armies gathered against Jerusalem, Jesus' reign over the nations of the earth, and the return of the nations to Jerusalem each year to worship the King during the Feast of Booths.

A great number of psalms also reference the return of Jesus to the earth just as they foretold the events of his First Coming. Psalms 93–100 encourage the world to joyfully worship and sing praise to the coming Messiah who reigns as king over the nations of the earth. The words of Psalm 95:2–4 encourage such thanksgiving and rejoicing:

> Let us come into his presence with thanksgiving; let us make a joyful noise to him with songs of praise! For the LORD is a great God, and a great King above all gods. In his hand are the depths of the earth; the heights of the mountains are his also.

Psalm 96:12 says that "all the trees of the forest" will "sing for joy" at the coming of Jesus to earth. Will the trees sing? In Romans 8:20–21,

Paul says that creation currently groans, waiting to be set free from its "bondage to corruption." What might it sound like to hear creation rejoicing and trees singing as they see their Creator returning in great glory? I'm not sure, but someday we'll know.

Why Is the Second Coming So Important?

"So, what does this mean to me?" you might ask. "Does Jesus' triumphant return really matter as I get up in the morning with sore knees and an achy back to face an uncertain world of overdue bills and injustice?"

Yes, it does!

1. ***The Second Coming signifies Jesus' ultimate victory over sin and death.*** I love the thought of Jesus' victorious and spectacular return to the world that rejected and crucified Him. At His Second Coming, Jesus will arrive with the majesty of a mighty and grand King. The world will mourn in recognition that their doom is sure (Revelation 1:7). The Jewish people will weep tears of repentance at the sight of their Messiah whom they once spurned.

If you're like me, you often become discouraged at the sight of evil and deceitful schemes enjoying great success in our world. We find ourselves repeatedly cancelled by a culture that rejects *all biblical* standards of morality and justice.

Jesus' future return to earth signifies the time when Psalm 46:10 will be true in our world. There, the Son of Korah wrote:

> Be still, and know that I am God. I will be exalted among the nations, I will be exalted in the earth.

Until then, we wait in stillness, contemplating God's sovereignty over all the affairs of humanity.

I cannot count the number of times when distressing news reports have caused me to turn to Psalm 46:10 followed by the reading of Psalm 37. Jesus is returning to this earth; those now promoting evil, violence, and world domination will meet their end. The Second Coming assures me of the defeat of all that's anti-God and wicked in our world.

2. The image of Jesus' future victory over the nations assures us of an eternity without pain and sorrow. We don't know where life will take us. We can be certain, however, that Jesus loves us more than we can understand and will not fail to safely bring us to His eternal kingdom. Jesus' power, as displayed at His Second Coming, assures us that nothing is impossible with Him. He is able to keep all His promises of a future life that will exceed all of our expectations. The promise of Revelation 21:4 will be ours for all eternity.

Life can be cruel and difficult; at times we all feel like throwing up our hands as we exclaim, "What's the use!?" However, this current existence is not the end of our story. Regardless of our current afflictions, we look forward to the time when we will share in Jesus' triumph over Satan and the nations that once rejected Him (and continue to do so).

24

We Will Reign with Christ

> The premillennial philosophy of history makes sense. It lays a biblical and rational basis for a truly optimistic view of human history. Furthermore, rightly apprehended, it has practical effects. It says that life here and now, in spite of the tragedy of sin, is nevertheless worth-while; and therefore all efforts to make it better are also worth-while. All the true values of human life will be preserved and carried over into the coming kingdom; nothing worth-while will be lost.
>
> ~Alva J. McClain, *The Greatness of the Kingdom*[95]

She had only a moments left in her brief life on earth.

As Christina sat cheerfully signing autographs after her concert in Orlando, Florida, she could not have known her killer was quietly approaching, gun in hand. The assassin despised her outspoken faith in Jesus and wanted to forever silence her voice.

I hadn't heard of Christina Grimmie until the shocking news broke of her murder on June 10, 2016. Soon afterward, I watched a video of her singing "In Christ Alone."

I will never forget the heartfelt emotion Christina put into these words:

No power of hell, no scheme of man,
Can ever pluck me from His hand;
Till He comes or calls me home,
here in the power of Christ I stand.[96]

Her passion and faith brought tears to my eyes as I thought about the violent end of her life against the backdrop of her love and passion for Jesus.

From a human perspective, Christina's murder seems like a senseless tragedy: a young, attractive, perky, and highly talented singer shot dead at the beginning of a promising career. How do we reconcile such an apparently meaningless death with our hope of forever? What's the purpose for all we endure during our short time on earth if our lives can end so quickly with an act of terror? Is this not an increasing possibility in the chaotic world in which we find ourselves?

On the other hand, what if our current lives as followers of Jesus are a preparation for the next? We know the Lord has a purpose for all He allows to come our way. But what if His objective for all the affliction and suffering and tragedy that He allows includes preparation for our roles when we reign with Him during the Millennium?

After Jesus comes for us, we will understand the Lord's forever purposes for *all* we experience, both the good, the not-so-good, and even the tragic events. I believe that even our darkest times will burst into bright, living color as the Lord reveals how they prepared us for our eternal position in His glorious kingdom.

Christina's beautiful voice will echo with praise for the Lord Jesus through all the years of the Millennium and then forevermore. *Her killer sought to forever silence her voice. He utterly failed. The only voice he silenced was his own.*

Christina Grimmie has only begun to sing for her Savior.

The Millennium

The word "millennium," which denotes one thousand years, comes from Revelation 20:1–10. In this passage, the Apostle John repeatedly refers to a thousand-year period during which Jesus binds Satan and reigns over the nations of the world. In verse 6, John says:

> Blessed and holy is the one who shares in the first resurrection! Over such the second death has no power, but they will be priests of God and of Christ, and they will reign with him for a thousand years.

While the apostle briefly mentions Jesus' millennial reign in Revelation 20, the Old Testament provides many more details of His rule over the nations in its repeated references to Jesus' Second Coming and His intermediate kingdom before the eternal state begins. Many chapters in the book of Isaiah, for example, describe the righteous reign of the Lord Jesus over the nations of the world. This will be a period of unparalleled harmony and rejoicing in the presence of our Savior (Isaiah 25:1–9).

In Psalm 96:10 we read:

> Say among the nations, "the LORD reigns! Yes, the world is established; it shall never be moved; he will judge the peoples with equity."

Jesus' return and reign will be such an occasion for great rejoicing on the earth that even nature will join in the celebration (see Psalm 96:11–13).

In Matthew 19:28–29, Jesus spoke about His future rule on the earth:

> Truly I tell you, at the renewal of all things, when the Son of Man sits on his glorious throne, you who have followed me will also sit on twelve thrones, judging the twelve tribes of Israel. And everyone who has left houses or brothers or sisters or father or mother or wife or children or fields for my sake will receive a hundred times as much and will inherit eternal life. (NIV)

Jesus describes His future kingdom as "the renewal of all things." Doesn't this give us a wondrous perspective of the future? Although we often experience loss and considerable grief in this life, Jesus promises us a time of "renewal," of restoration; He will make up for the losses we sustain and reward our faithfulness.

For those of us in Christ, afflictions, sorrow, aging, cancer, and death (even tragic ones such as Christina Grimmie's) do not signify the end of our story or our usefulness to the Savior. Regardless of our fate here below, we await the Lord's wondrous "renewal of all things" when we will understand the many things that now make no sense.

Forget the "bucket list." For each adventure or wondrous scene in nature we do not experience here below, we will have at least a thousand more opportunities in the coming kingdom and then in eternity. Please understand that I absolutely love to travel and see the various wonders of God's creation, and I'm happy for those who are able to do this beyond what I have been able. My point is that I feel no remorse for what I'm not able to enjoy in this lifetime because I know something of what lies ahead for me during the Millennium (and eternal state as well).

I have no "bucket list" item other than to be alive at the time of the Rapture.

Joseph and the Millennium

Several years ago, I watched the Genesis account of the biography of Joseph portrayed in a TNT mini-series. The show brought to life many aspects of his bondage and imprisonment as well as his spectacular rise to power. The writers of this production did a great job of following the biblical text. As it brought Joseph's story to living color, it also spoke to me concerning our participation in the future millennial reign of Jesus.

What if someone had told Joseph as he trudged—bound in chains from neck to feet—across a hot desert that he would someday rule alongside Pharaoh of Egypt? Wouldn't he have thought that person insane? Yet, by the end of the story, we see that was God's purpose behind all the many afflictions Joseph experienced. He rose from slavery and years in prison to become the second most powerful man in the world at that time.

The Lord used Joseph's betrayal by his brothers, his time in the household of Potiphar, and his imprisonment as training ground for what He had planned for him. Joseph learned wise stewardship as the head of Potiphar's household and the value of faithfulness as Potiphar's wife tempted him and then falsely accused him. In prison, Joseph trusted God's ongoing presence as he interpreted dreams for the baker and cupbearer and waited for what must have seemed a lifetime or his situation to improve.

The Lord intertwined all these experiences to position and prepare Joseph for when he would rule over all of Egypt alongside Pharaoh.

Do you see the parallel for us? Like Joseph, we will someday see how the Lord's purposes in all our experiences and suffering fit together for His unique plans for us in His kingdom during the time we will reign with Him.

We also see this relationship between our current lives and eternity in the parable of the talents, in which Jesus gives His followers kingdom responsibilities based on their faithfulness to Him (Matthew 25:14–30). The Apostle Paul wrote about the Judgment Seat of Christ; there He will examine our faithfulness in serving Him (1 Corinthians 3:10–15; 2 Corinthians 5:10). Our rewards for faithful service will determine our place in Jesus' kingdom.

It's no wonder that Satan hates biblical teaching regarding the Millennium and does everything in his power to twist the supporting biblical prophecies through allegorical interpretations.

The prospect of our future reign with Jesus in His earthly kingdom radically transforms our thinking regarding the ups and downs of this life. It tips the balance scale dramatically in favor of eternity.

Of course, the Lord uses our trials and afflictions to promote our spiritual growth and enable us to better serve others in the here and now. But oh, what wonder to contemplate how He might fit everything together for our future roles in His millennial kingdom!

The One who now sees all our suffering and the many tears that flow down our cheeks also looks ahead to the time He will bring us home to the place He's preparing for us. The One who sees our current afflictions knows precisely how He will use our experiences along with our gifts and abilities in His kingdom.

The night that I sat alongside the church at 4 a.m., I thought the Lord had abandoned me. Why would He let me suffer so much without riding on a white horse to my rescue? Now however, I realize that He waited to intervene for my maturity and growth. Additionally, He looked ahead to how He would later bless and use me as He watched the tears roll down my cheeks. It was painful, but Jesus knew He was preparing me to serve Him both at a future time in this life as well as in His kingdom.

The Lord who guides us through suffering and affliction also sees how He is going to use that for our future benefit in eternity. Doesn't that encourage our hearts in the midst of the difficulties we so often face?

God's love is beyond amazing! It's beyond our comprehension that He would take sinners, redeem us by the blood of His Son, immerse us in Christ's death and resurrection, and then allow us to share in Jesus' triumph and someday rule alongside Him in His kingdom.

25

We Will Spend Eternity in Paradise

The most ordinary moment on the New Earth will be greater than the most perfect moments in this life—those experiences you wanted to bottle or hang on to but couldn't. It *can* get better, far better, than this—*and it will.* Life on the New Earth will be like sitting in front of the fire with family and friends, basking in the warmth, laughing uproariously, dreaming of the adventures to come—and then going out and **living** those adventures together. With no fear that life will ever end or that tragedy will descend like a dark cloud. With no fear that dreams will be shattered or relationships broken.

~Randy Alcorn, *Heaven*[97]

He was the most joyous and Spirit-filled believer I had seen. Though it was many decades ago, I remember the delight that beamed from Paul Lundgren's face as he sang one Sunday evening at our church.

Years earlier, a traffic accident had left Paul paralyzed from the waist down. That didn't deter him, however, from cheerfully singing and talking at length about his future in paradise when he would walk on streets of gold.

As a high schooler who cherished any opportunity to play baseball, tennis, or basketball (despite an overall lack of athleticism), his cheerfulness baffled me. He couldn't do what I enjoyed the most, yet I had never seen anyone so jubilant or so in love with Jesus. How could someone confined to a wheelchair for the rest of his life exude such delight and confident hope?

Paul's upbeat attitude in spite of his paralysis stemmed from his biblical view of eternity, from a two-world perspective. He allowed his anticipation of future bliss and wholeness to flow back into his everyday life and his ministry of singing. He valued eternal glory over his temporary affliction—which, though severe, did not cloud his vision of paradise and the joy he felt because of his hope.

To this day, the sight of him exuberantly singing from his wheelchair humbles me. He knew what it meant to value eternity over his suffering and physical limitations.

Paul Lungren's witness resonates for us to this day: Regardless of our circumstances on earth, our life in eternity will be far, far better, and that makes it possible to let our future bliss flow back into our lives even in the midst of adversity.

Eternity

In his book *Desire*, John Eldredge quoted physicist Blaise Pascal:

> Our imagination so powerfully magnifies time, by continual reflections upon it, and so diminishes eternity…for want of reflection…we make a nothing of eternity and an eternity of nothing.[98]

Eldredge expanded on that sentiment with these words:

> We make a nothing of eternity by enlarging the significance of this life and by diminishing the reality of what the next life is all about.[99]

We all fight the tendency to value our current aspirations above eternal outcomes, don't we? I know I do. It's so easy to become preoccupied with this life at the expense of an eternal focus, and in doing so "make a nothing of eternity and an eternity of nothing." That's why the specifics of our hope matter; they not only assure us of a sudden departure to meet Jesus in the air, a celebration in heaven, and our reign with Jesus in His kingdom, but also keep our hearts focused on these things.

Isaiah 25:6–9 paints a picture of a bountiful party the Lord will host for us in eternity:

> On this mountain the Lord of hosts will make for all peoples a feast of rich food, a feast of well-aged wine, of rich food full of marrow, of aged wine well refined. And he will swallow up on this mountain the covering that is cast over all peoples, the veil that is spread over all nations. He will swallow up death forever; and the Lord God will wipe away tears from all faces, and the reproach of his people he will take away from all the earth for the Lord has spoken. It will be said on that day, "Behold, this is our God; we have waited for him, that he might save us. This is the Lord; we have waited for him; let us be glad and rejoice in his salvation."

Does a hearty feast with the best food imaginable and great wine come to your mind first when you think of eternity? Do you envision Jesus preparing such a lavish banquet for you? Yet God's Word promises the Lord will someday host just such a party where we will celebrate His victory over sin, death, sorrow, and so much more.

Can you sense the sheer delight in the words of Isaiah 25:9? Someday we will be the ones triumphantly exclaiming, "This is the Lord; we have waited for him; let us be glad and rejoice in his salvation." We will forever praise the Lord for what He has done for us, but in addition to that, we revel in his goodness as He displays his kindness toward us throughout all eternity (Ephesians 2:7).

The New Earth

My eternal focus did not include a restored earth until I read John Eldredge's book *Desire* several years ago and began to contemplate the new earth that the Apostle John mentions in Revelation 21:1. Eldredge said:

> How wondrous this will be! Creation can be so breathtaking *now*. What shall it be like when it is released to its full glory?[100]

Our view of eternity can be so dismal compared to what God reveals in His Word. Clothed with resurrected and imperishable bodies, we will have all eternity to explore the wonders of a restored creation and universe as we marvel at its breathtaking views. Although we don't know all the details of our eternal existence, Scripture's depictions of it in Revelation 21–22 are far more than enough for us to cease making "a nothing of eternity and an eternity of nothing."

When we consider what the Bible reveals about eternity, our joyous anticipation grows. Regardless of our fate in this life, we know a much better existence will begin the moment Jesus' comes for us. Our best moments, and best meals for that matter, will not happen before then. We will enjoy our most satisfying pleasures in eternity.

The New Jerusalem

In Revelation 21–22, John describes heaven as the joining of the New Jerusalem to God's newly restored earth. In eternity, we will enjoy all the benefits of the most beautiful city we can ever imagine along with the new earth. When we think of the paradise that awaits us, it's not just one or the other.

John provides a spectacular *eyewitness* account of the New Jerusalem. Let's look at a few of its features.

1. God dwelling with His people: The Lord's presence on earth via the New Jerusalem will exceed all we can imagine about it. In our resurrected bodies, we will see God in all His glory within the towering walls of the New Jerusalem.

Randy Alcorn, in his book *Heaven*, describes the Lord's presence in this way:

> The presence of God is the essence of Heaven (just as the absence of God is the essence of Hell). Because God is beautiful beyond measure, if we knew nothing more than that Heaven was God's dwelling place, it would be more than enough. The best part of life on the New Earth will be enjoying God's presence, having him actually dwelling among us (Rev. 22:14).[101]

2. Beauty beyond all that we can imagine: As John watched the New Jerusalem descend from heaven, he described its appearance as "having the glory of God, its radiance like a most rare jewel, like a jasper, clear as crystal" (21:11). Later, the apostle listed all the jewels adorning its foundation and described its street as being of pure gold (21:18–21).

Picture the most beautiful place you've seen either in person or in a fictional account; the splendor of our heavenly dwelling place will far surpass that. Even the most fanciful depictions of towns in futuristic movies will not come close to the magnificence of our eternal home.

Alcorn gives this answer to those who compare the New Jerusalem to earthly cities and hence lack excitement about residing in another city:

> But this city will be different—it will have all the advantages we associate with earthly cities but none of the disadvantages. The city will be filled with natural wonders, magnificent architecture, thriving culture—but it will have no crime, pollution, sirens, traffic fatalities, garbage, or homelessness. It will truly be Heaven on Earth.[102]

3. The absence of pain and sorrow: The Apostle John tells us that evil will not exist in the New Jerusalem or anywhere on the new earth for that matter. Sickness, death, sorrow, tears, pain, and certainly crime will be things of the distant past:

> He will wipe away every tear from their eyes, and death shall be no more, neither shall there be mourning, nor crying, nor pain anymore, for the former things have passed away. (21:4).

Pastor and commentator John MacArthur wrote this about the absence of pain and sorrow:

> What it declares is the absence of anything to be sorry about—no sadness, no disappointment, no pain. There will be no tears of misfortune, tears over lost love, tears of remorse, tears of regret, tears over the death of loved ones, or tears for any other reason.
>
> Another dramatic difference from the present world will be that in heaven there will no longer be any death (cf. Isa. 25:8). The greatest curse of human existence will be no more. "Death,"

as Paul promised, "is swallowed up in victory (1 Cor. 15:54). Both Satan, who had the power of death (Heb. 2:14), and death itself will have been cast into the lake of fire (20:10, 14).[103]

4. **Residence of the saints of all ages:** The New Jerusalem will have twelve gates on which will appear "the names of the twelve tribes of the sons of Israel" (21:12). The walls of the city will have twelve foundations, each listing one of "the twelve names of the twelve apostles of the Lamb" (21:14). The redeemed of all the ages will reside there.

Imagine having a conversation with Joseph, or perhaps with King David or the Apostle Paul. Oh, the questions we might ask them. Perhaps Jonah will tell us what it was like to be inside the belly of a great fish. Joshua could provide a firsthand account of watching the walls of Jericho tumble to the ground. Peter might recount for us his experience of the angel leading him out of prison.

Hebrews 12:22 reveals that his heavenly Jerusalem will be home to the angels as well:

> But you have come to Mount Zion and to the city of the living God, the heavenly Jerusalem, and to innumerable angels in festal gathering.

What an exciting and joyous picture of our eternal home. Together with the saints of all the ages and with the angels, we will forever celebrate God's grace and enjoy life to its fullness with God Himself, who will dwell with us.

5. **Incredible dimensions:** The apostle also provides the measurements of the New Jerusalem in 21:15–17. Imagine a cube 1,380 miles long on each side and 1,380 miles tall. If superimposed upon the United States, it would take up well over half of the country with just its width and length. It's understandable why the angel took John to a high mountain; he needed such a wide perspective to see something that huge.

Wouldn't you expect the place that houses the throne of God, the angels, and the redeemed of all the ages to be so immense? Doesn't John's depiction of the city fit with the grandeur and redeeming purposes of our great God?

We have no reason to doubt John's eyewitness account regarding the enormity of the New Jerusalem as some mistakenly do. It will be a physical and tangible city of great proportions. Why would we expect anything less?

6. Accessible from the earth: John adds this interesting detail to his description:

> By its light will the nations walk, and the kings of the earth will bring their glory into it, and its gates will never be shut by day—and there will be no night there. (Revelation 21:24–25).

In eternity, people will come and go from the New Jerusalem. I believe we will have a home in heaven's capital with unlimited access to explore the wondrous beauty of God's creation.

Furthermore, is it too much to imagine that we might have more than one residence in eternity? I have no biblical basis for this, but it's possible we may have one home in the New Jerusalem and another somewhere on the earth for carrying out our official duties of reigning with Christ in eternity.

A Warning

Our residence in the eternal state, which will consist of the new earth and the spectacular New Jerusalem, will NOT come as a reward for our good behavior. It's not at all based on our morality, ability to keep the law, avoidance of sin, church attendance, parents' faith, or even sincerity.

We cannot gain admittance to this eternal paradise through religious behavior or any good works. That's impossible. The Lord reserves this eternal paradise exclusively for the redeemed of all the ages, those He saves via His death on the cross. It's only a time of triumph because we share in Christ's victory over sin, death, and the grave.

Jesus is the *only* path to eternal life: He said, "I am the way, the truth, and the life. No one comes to the Father except through me" (John 14:6). Despite the clarity of His words, many assume there are other ways to heaven. They do not exist.

In Ephesians 2:8–9, Paul tells us that God saves us by His grace through faith. It's never about our works; we will never have an opportunity to boast about our goodness as having anything to do with salvation.

If you've never trusted the Lord as your Savior, please do so today. Tomorrow, it may be too late. Jesus is the only One who can take away your sins and exchange them for His very own righteousness. Second Corinthians 5:21 says:

> For our sake he made him to be sin who knew no sin, so that in him we might become the righteousness of God.

With such a prize ahead for those who know the Lord, it's no wonder that Jesus said in Luke 10:20:

> Nevertheless, do not rejoice in this, that the spirits are subject to you, but rejoice that your names are written in heaven.

Because our names appear above, we will someday enjoy the new earth and the New Jerusalem forever and ever.

Conclusion

One Minute to Midnight

> Besides this you know the time, that the hour has come for you to wake from sleep. For salvation is nearer to us now than when we first believed. The night is far gone; the day is at hand. So then let us cast off the works of darkness and put on the armor of light.
>
> –The Apostle Paul, Romans 13:11–12

Is this it? Are we living in the very last moments before the Rapture? Isn't the coming Tribulation coming at our world like an out-of-control locomotive? Do we not see the Antichrist's kingdom beginning to take shape at this moment?

Far too many Christians answer "no" to these questions; they offer an assortment of reasons for their response, such as: "We've seen lawlessness, wars, chaos, economic downturns, and pandemics before in history; today is no different. We've been hearing about Jesus' return for decades; our grandparents watched for the Rapture, but He hasn't yet come. Why should we expect Him to appear now?" They may end with this remark, "Sure, it's bad, but this is not the end of the age."

So yes, people today in large numbers ridicule the belief that we live in the last days of human history as we know it; they accuse those of us who do believe that of interpreting prophecy based on current news, of reading the Bible in one hand and a newspaper in the other. I believe that just the opposite is true; we know what headlines to expect because the Lord spoke of this time in Scripture.

As we look at our world through the lens of biblical prophecy, it leads to one conclusion: It's one minute to midnight, and the clock is ticking.

What Makes Today Different?

Because so many believers today doubt that that we live in the last moments before Rapture and seven-year Tribulation, it's important that we answer this question: Why does our time in history differ from any other since the start of the Church?

1. The Rebirth of Israel as a Nation

Sir Isaac Newton (1642–1726), based on his extensive study of the books of Daniel and Revelation, believed that Israel must exist as a nation before the Jesus returned to earth—and he even predicted that it would happen.[104] He correctly assumed that the fulfillment of many of the end-time prophecies in the Bible necessitated Israel's existence. Premillennialists during the first half of the twentieth century also predicted its reemergence as a country, and then it happened!

The prophet Isaiah asked long ago, "Shall a land be born in one day? Shall a nation be brought forth in one moment?" (Isaiah 66:8). The answer is an astounding "Yes!" On May 14, 1948, God fulfilled this impossible-sounding prophecy: Israel became a nation in a day. One cannot overstate its significance or dismiss this amazing miracle as a mere coincidence. Israel's supernatural existence not only fulfilled prophecy, but it also set the stage for the fulfillment of many other end-time prophecies.

The regathering of the Jewish people back to the land, as we see today, had to happen before the Tribulation period and the revival of faith that happens at Jesus' return (Zechariah 12:10.) This, however, is just the start of what makes our day unique prophetically and markedly different from any previous time in history.

2. The Third Jewish Temple

The biblical sequence of events leading up to the Second Coming also necessitates that the Third Temple exist in Jerusalem by the midpoint of the seven-year Tribulation. It's at the halfway point of the Tribulation that the Antichrist desecrates the Jewish Temple and begins his deadly rampage against the Jewish people (Daniel 9:27; Matthew 24:15–20; 2 Thessalonians 2:3–8). According to Scripture, the nation must complete construction of the Third Temple during the first half of this coming time of judgment on the earth.

In chapter 8, I provided quotes from Irenaeus in the second century AD and from Isaac Newton regarding their predictions that the Antichrist would defile a Third Temple during the Tribulation. Today, we see this taking shape as never before. The Temple Institute in Israel has been working on this for over thirty years, and the Israeli government is already drafting infrastructure plans for when it becomes a reality.

The Temple Institute has already recreated all the Temple furnishings except for the ark of the covenant. They have secured the architectural plans for the future structure and are ready to start construction as soon as they have the needed permission. Not only have they recreated the clothing for the priests based on the requirements outlined in the Old Testament, but they are also training Levites to serve as priests in the Temple.[105]

3. The New World Order

As we've touched on earlier, the powers behind the World Economic Forum (WEF) refer to the coming world government as the Great Reset. This wording sounds far less frightening than the Marxists and totalitarian government they plan to impose on the world to enslave the people of all the nations.

Why do many students of prophecy believe that the Great Reset will most likely lead to the final form of the fourth beast? Because it has many of the characteristics of the regime that will ruthlessly dominate the world during the Tribulation under the direction of the Antichrist. A cursory look of the WEF website might make one think they seek to establish a utopia on the earth. But as one reads through the details of what they propose, it becomes apparent that they advocate a Marxist world order.

Peter Koenig, a geopolitical analyst and a former senior economist at the World Bank and the World Health Organization (WHO), wrote this about the agenda of the elite such as Klaus Schwab, the founder and head of the WEF:

> We have become enslaved to the Beast. The Beast calls the shots on boom or bust of our economies, on who should be shackled by debt, when and where a pandemic should break out, and on the conditions of surviving the pandemic, for example, social confinement. And to top it all off—the instruments the Beast uses, very cleverly, are a tiny-tiny invisible enemy, called a virus, and a huge but also invisible monster, called FEAR. That keeps us off the street, off reunions with our friends, and off our social entertainment, theatre, sports, or a picnic in the park.
>
> Soon the Beast will decide who will live and who will die, literally—if we let it. This may be not far away. Another wave of pandemic and people may beg, yell and scream for a vaccine, for

> their death knell, and for the super bonanza of Big Pharma—and towards the objectives of the eugenicists blatantly roaming the world—see this. There is still time to collectively say NO. Collectively and solidarity.[106]

I find it quite remarkable that Peter Koenig—who, to my knowledge, is not a believer in Jesus or biblical prophecy—uses the same term that Daniel and the Apostle John did to describe the coming kingdom that will dominate the world during the Tribulation.

I admit it's not easy reading about the demonic, sinister, and deadly motives of those who seek to enslave the world's population in such a way. Despite the warnings, many people in our world remain deep in delusion, believing that, this time, socialism will morph to their long-awaited utopia.

4. COVID-19 and the Great Reset

Klaus Schwab said this regarding COVID-19 in July of 2020: "The pandemic represents a rare but narrow window of opportunity to reflect, reimagine, and reset our world."[107] The "China Virus" has become the springboard through which globalists such as Schwab seek to the implement the Great Reset.

The globalists of our day are evil beyond what most of us can imagine; they are most certainly not above the furthering of their agenda through worldwide suffering and death, such as what has happened as the result of the China Virus. In John 8:44, Jesus describes the devil, the inspiration and power behind these elite globalists, as a "murderer from the beginning" and one who "has nothing to do with the truth." I believe these elite purposely weaponized the coronavirus by making it much more contagious and deadly before releasing it to the world.

Peter Koenig wrote the following about the planning behind COVID-19:

> We are indeed living in a very dystopian world, in a Twilight Zone. Once you see it—then you don't; the disaster planned upon us. Does anyone still doubt that it is NOT a coincidence that all the 193 UN member countries were at once befallen by this mysterious virus, and that all at once had to "perform" their first lockdown? Namely mid-March 2020? ALL countries? On commando.
>
> Doesn't this look like there is another motive behind?
>
> Is it a coincidence, that there is the 2010 Rockefeller Report (focusing on the Lockstep scenario) predicting ten years later as the first step in their nefarious 4-phase plan, the "Lockstep Scenario"—which is exactly what we are experiencing now; the entire western civilization is walking in lockstep, as we are told.[108]

Though not a believer, Koenig recognizes what most pastors and Christians today refuse to acknowledge. He sees the agenda behind COVID-19 and recognizes its purpose in bringing in the Great Reset or coming New World Order.

The globalists planned the disaster we know as COVID-19, and it's performing the desired function of pushing the world toward their objective. Aided by a willing media, the elite have created a climate of panic in our world that will cause many to readily accept a global government that appears to possess the answers to all the problems that people now face.

The virus is real; it has caused many deaths and much suffering throughout the world. Please know that when I refer to COVID-19 as a "plandemic," I am not at all minimizing the toll it has taken on those who have suffered greatly from it or lost loved ones because of it.

The COVID-19 "vaccines" have resulted in the deaths of thousands. I am personally aware of two who have died and others who have greatly suffered directly as a result of these mRNA injections masquerading as vaccines.

5. Technology That Makes the Mark of the Beast Possible

The emergence of artificial intelligence (AI) during the past few years also makes today much different than any other time since the time of Christ. AI technology makes it possible for the Antichrist to control all the buying and selling worldwide exactly as described in Revelation 13:15–17:

> And it was allowed to give breath to the image of the beast, so that the image of the beast might even speak and might cause those who would not worship the image of the beast to be slain. Also it causes all, both small and great, both rich and poor, both free and slave, to be marked on the right hand or the forehead, so that no one can buy or sell unless he has the mark, that is, the name of the beast or the number of its name.

I recently watched a video where Tom Hughes and Billy Crone, both senior pastors and popular speakers on the matter of biblical prophecy, discussed how AI along with the 5G network makes it possible for one person, the Antichrist, to control the buying and selling taking place in the world.[109] Crone, who has done extensive research on this, likened the development of AI to the rebirth of Israel in terms of prophetic significance, because now, as never before, the world possesses the means for the Antichrist and False Prophet to fulfill what John wrote in Revelation 13:15–18 concerning the mark of the Beast.

Apart from AI, the Antichrist would require a huge number of workers throughout the world to control all commerce. This technology, once fully in place, will allow him to do this without support on such a grand scale.

The literal interpretation of Revelation 13, accepted by faith in previous generations of Bible students of prophecy, is fast becoming a reality.

6. Deception

When the disciples asked Jesus about "the sign of your coming and of the end of the age," His first words were these, "See that no one leads you astray" (Matthew 24:3–4). In the same discourse, Jesus also warns about "false teachers" seeking to lead others "astray" (Matthew 24:11, 24). In 2 Thessalonians 2:7–12, the Apostle Paul writes about the deception that will characterize the Antichrist and his time.

Do we not see this happening everywhere in our world today? In just the past year, we've seen "big tech" censor truth on social media as never before. Never before has it been so difficult to distinguish the truth from the abundance of lies and misinformation that daily confront us.

Yes, there have been other times of mass deception such as we see today in the United States and throughout our world. The disinformation campaign in Germany that led to the rise of Adolf Hitler and the Third Reich is very much like what we see happening today in the United States.

The difference between Germany in the past century and today is threefold. First, we have all the *other* signs of the last days converging at this time. Second, *the deception is happening worldwide, rather than in just one country*. And third, with the advances in technology, those who stamp out the truth have more effective means of doing so than existed in the lead up to World War II.

7. The Signs of Matthew 24

The signs Jesus gave in Matthew 24:3–14 continue to increase in intensity and frequency like "birth pains," just as He said they would in the days preceding His return to earth. Jesus' first words typify today's world: "See that no one leads you astray" (v. 4). We live in a day when deception is king. It's more than difficult than ever for believers to discover truth in the overabundance of information available.

As for earthquakes (Matthew 24:7), they have increased in intensity and frequency just within the past seven days, as of the time I'm editing this chapter (February 17, 2021). A total of 252 earthquakes that registered above 4.0 on the Richter Scale have occurred in just the past week.

The signs Jesus gave of the days leading up to His return read like the news headlines of our day. They again confirm that this is indeed a day like no other.

These signs are just a few of the many that are converging like at no other time in history. It's not an exaggeration to say it's one minute to midnight on God's prophetic calendar.

Now Is the Time

If you haven't yet done so, now is the time to align your hopes and dreams with the reality that you may not have tomorrow. Regardless of your belief concerning the Rapture, the storm clouds threatening our world grow darker by the moment and threaten the future of everyone on earth. Peter Koenig writes article after article warning of the dire consequences of the COVID-19 vaccine and of the coming New World Order that he believes will enslave the people of the world. David Horowitz, an atheist, repeatedly warns believers in America that they will face intense and likely violent persecution in the months and years ahead.

Unfortunately, these secular writers see what so many pastors do not. Despite their lack of belief in the Bible, they warn people of a future that sounds remarkably similar to what John witnessed at the time he wrote the book of Revelation.

For those of you outside of Christ, ***now is the time*** to place your faith in Him. John 3:16 says:

> For God so loved the world, that he gave his only Son, that whoever believes in him should not perish but have eternal life.

Just hours before His death on cross in our place, Jesus said:

> I am the way, the truth, and the life. No one comes to the Father except through me. (John 14:6)

Apart from faith in Jesus, you will face the terrors of the coming Tribulation if you are alive at that time, and you will face an eternity torment away from God's presence.

Ephesians 2:8–9 says:

> For by grace you have been saved through faith. And this is not your own doing; it is the gift of God, not a result of works, so that no one may boast.

We need God's grace, because apart from Him we are all sinners in need in of forgiveness. Romans 3:23 says "for all have sinned and fall short of the glory of God."

The good news is that, in Jesus, "we have redemption through his blood, the forgiveness of our trespasses, according to the riches of his grace" (Ephesians 1:7). Christ paid the debt for sins on the cross, and because of the blood He shed, we receive forgiveness of sins through Him.

I love the simplicity of the Apostle John's words in 1 John 5:11–12:

> And this is the testimony, that God gave us eternal life, and this life is in his Son. Whoever has the Son has life; whoever does not have the Son of God does not have life.

Knowing Jesus as your Savior equals eternal life.

Have you put your trust in Him? Have you called out to Jesus in faith, asking Him to forgive your sins? Does your hope of eternal life depend 100 percent on the Lord, and on Him alone? Please put your faith in Christ while you have time.

For those of you securely in the arms of the Savior, ***now is the time*** to recognize that you may soon be with Jesus in paradise via the Rapture. ***Now is the time*** to hold your dreams and aspirations for the future loosely in your hands.

I'm not saying it's wrong to make plans, set goals, dream, or carry on with our lives, but we must do so with hearts and minds aware of the growing storm clouds that at some point may threaten our livelihoods and perhaps our lives if the Rapture doesn't occur first.

I don't know when the Rapture will occur or the date the Tribulation will start, but I see what is happening throughout the world, and I recognize a multitude of signs that tell us we live in the last days of human history as we know it.

Now is the time to recognize the fleeting nature of our current lives versus the eternal nature of our resurrected bodies in which we will forever enjoy the sights and pleasures of the new earth and the New Jerusalem.

Our exciting and eternal adventure starts with the Rapture, and it is coming soon. We will surely share in Christ's triumph over all His foes and forever reign with Him in the Millennium—and after that in the eternal state where the joys of exploring God's creation will never end and our amazement of seeing the New Jerusalem and our God will continue for all eternity.

We will share in Jesus' future triumph over sin and death. We will inherit a kingdom and reign with Him forevermore.

Maranatha!

Appendix

No Saint Left Behind

Another errant teaching has become popular today; theologians refer to it as the "partial-Rapture" theory. Those with this view believe that only those who are watching for the Lord's return or are ready for it will depart to heaven with Jesus when He comes for His Church. Those not walking with the Lord or not watching at the time will go through the terrible Tribulation for further purification—a purgatory of sorts for living saints.

Will Jesus leave true believers behind when He comes for Cis Church? ***Absolutely not!*** I strongly disagree with this teaching for reasons I will expound upon in this appendix.

Please note that I am referring to those who are truly in Christ. Many who profess faith in Jesus will miss out on the Rapture because they don't truly know Him as their Savior. Others who rely on good works, church attendance, or the "Sinner's Prayer" rather than the Lord for their salvation will also miss out on the Rapture.

I believe that *all* living saints whom the Savior has redeemed will meet the Lord in the air when He appears to take His Church back to His Father's house, no exceptions!

Let me explain why I have such confidence.

The Partial-Rapture Theory Contradicts the Gospel

The partial-Rapture teaching contradicts the clear saving message of the gospel.

Ephesians 2:8–9 says:

> For by grace you have been saved through faith. And this is not your own doing; it is the gift of God, not a result of works, so that no one may boast.

We receive eternal life by grace through faith, not because of our works or faithfulness. The Lord regenerates us and gives us the faith to believe. From start to finish, our salvation is all about Jesus and the Spirit's saving and preserving work inside us (Titus 3:4–7).

If our lack of watchfulness or devotion can prevent our participation in the Rapture, this means we must add something to Jesus' work on our behalf to confirm our worthiness for our inclusion. This adds *works* to our salvation and provides a reason for boasting for those who return to heaven with Jesus. Both of these elements contradict what's said in Ephesians 2:8–9.

American evangelist D. L. Moody once said, "It takes the same grace to keep us saved as it does to save us." Our salvation is all grace; works play no part whatsoever in our initial salvation or in our final glorification. The reception of our glorified bodies at the moment of the Rapture no more depends on our good behavior than our justification when we turn to Christ.

Second Corinthians 5:21 says:

> For our sake he made him to be sin who knew no sin, so that in him we might become the righteousness of God.

The basis of our salvation is the righteousness of Jesus. As believers, we stand "holy and blameless before" God simply because of our position in Christ (Ephesians 1:3–4). The One who made spiritually dead "children of wrath" His own dear sons and daughters (see Ephesians 2:1–7) will not fail to complete His saving work in us when He comes to take us home.

Since all New Testament saints stand before God in the righteousness of Jesus, how can we assume the presence of any separation at the time of Jesus' appearing? *If we are all "holy and blameless" before Him, wherein lies the basis for any distinction among us?*

Partial Rapture Contradicts Paul's Promise in 1 Thessalonians 5:9–10

The teaching of a partial Rapture contradicts the words of 1 Thessalonians 5:9–10. There Paul writes:

> For God has not destined us for wrath, but to obtain salvation through our Lord Jesus Christ, who died for us so that whether we are awake or asleep we might live with him.

The context tells us this wrath must belong to the Day of the Lord or what we refer to as the Tribulation; it's not a reference to the punishment of hell, but to the future time of God's judgments during the Tribulation.

Paul tells us that when Jesus returns, He will deliver both those who are "awake or asleep" from God's wrath. Since Paul just wrote about the Rapture, including both living saints and the "dead in Christ" (1 Thessalonians 4:16–17), many carry that same meaning to 1 Thessalonians 5:10, thinking it refers to dead and living saints, but this is not the case.

In 1 Thessalonians 5:10, the apostle is *not* making a distinction between living and dead saints as he did in chapter 4; he's contrasting saints who are walking as children of light versus those who are not. He's promising that neither group will miss out on the Rapture.

I know this may sound shocking to some, but Paul's choice of words in verse 10 confirms that he's referring to the two groups of believers he described in verses 4–8.

The Greek verb for "awake" in verse 10 is *gregoreo,* a word that denotes moral alertness. In verses 4–8, Paul uses it along with soberness to portray the idea of temperance in our walk with the Lord versus that of drunkenness or carelessness, which is the conduct of those who walk in darkness. "So then let us not sleep, as others do, but let us keep awake and be sober" (v. 6). Jesus used *gregoreo* in Matthew 24:42 and Mark 13:35 in the sense of being watchful for His return.

The idea of being awake in 1 Thessalonians 5:10 denotes a spiritual condition; it doesn't have the connotation of being alive versus that of being physically dead.

What about those whom Paul characterizes as being "asleep" in verse 10?

The word Paul uses for believers who are "asleep" in 5:10 is *katheudo*. This word almost always refers to someone who is physically asleep rather than dead. Of the twenty-two times this word appears in the New Testament, it only once refers to someone who had died, and then Jesus used the word to refer to the girl he intended to raise from the dead. In 1 Thessalonians 4:17, Paul uses a different Greek word, *zao,* to refer to living saints at the time of the Rapture.

In the context of 1 Thessalonians 5:4–8, Paul uses *katheudo* with moral implications warning believers not to fall asleep in their walk with the Lord and behave as those outside of Christ (vv. 6–7). It's the opposite of the sober saint or the one Paul characterizes as *gregoreo,* or awake. The word denotes the spiritual condition of being asleep; it doesn't refer to those who have ceased breathing. In the context of verse 10, *katheudo* refers to someone who has become careless in his or her walk with the Lord.

Based on the context and the Paul's change of vocabulary from chapter 4, the sense of 1 Thessalonians 5:10 is that when Jesus returns for His Church, He will Rapture those who are alert spiritually as well as those who have fallen asleep in their walk with Him.

The promise of 1 Thessalonians 5:10 is that our inclusion in the Rapture doesn't depend upon our behavior or our watchfulness at the moment Jesus appears; it depends solely upon whether or not we belong to Christ.

First John 5:10–12 spells out the only condition for our inclusion in the Rapture. If we belong to Jesus, He will take us to glory regardless of our behavior at the moment He appears! On the other hand, if we don't have Jesus in our life, we will remain earthbound regardless of the great many works we may have done and in spite of even having lived an outstanding moral life.

Please understand I'm not saying that our behavior doesn't matter. It absolutely does! I am saying that those who teach the doctrine of a partial Rapture advance a doctrine that contradicts the heart of the gospel as well as Paul's specific promise in 1 Thessalonians 5:10.

The bottom line is this: No matter where true saints of the Lord are in their walk with Him at the time of the Rapture, they will receive glorified bodies when He comes for His Church. Regardless of their watchfulness at the time of Jesus' appearing, they will participate in the Rapture.

I don't have all the answers, but I know two things for sure. Frist, God's justification of the sinner is permanent and leads to glorification (Romans 8:30–39). Nothing can break that chain.

Second, Jesus will not leave behind any saint who possesses His righteousness because of God's irreversible verdict in justifying us when we were sinners.

No true saint will miss out in the Rapture.

The Dangers

I believe the doctrine of a partial Rapture is dangerous because it adds works to grace and insults the righteousness of Christ.

Christ's sacrifice on our behalf is enough and always will be. Those in Christ don't need further purification; we are already "holy and blameless before him" (Ephesians 1:4). We cannot improve our standing before the Lord, nor can we diminish it!

There is no purgatory (further cleansing of sin) for those in Christ whether alive or already with the Lord; Jesus will not leave any of His own behind when He comes for His Church.

The cross is enough!

Another danger of the partial-Rapture teaching is that it has the potential to deceive those who remain on the earth after Jesus' appearing. If they believe their lack of faithfulness or watchfulness caused them to miss out on their trip to paradise, they will blame their behavior rather than their unregenerate state. In other words, they might seek to remedy the problem with good works that will not bring them any closer the saving grace they'll so desperately need for their eternal salvation.

The advocates of the partial-Rapture doctrine don't take into consideration those who have died in Christ. They only refer to the worthiness of living believers to take part in the Rapture and thereby assume all New Testament saints already in heaven with Jesus will participate. Indeed, they cannot suggest a further purifying for this later group without venturing into the realm of purgatory, for which there is absolutely no biblical support.

One the one hand, those who limit the Rapture to those walking faithfully with the Lord say that some believers will need the Tribulation for purification purposes. On the other hand, they cannot say anything similar about those who have gone before us with delving into the realm of heresy.

In 1 Thessalonians 4:13–18, Paul settled the matter concerning the loved ones in the church there who had already died. They will absolutely not miss out on the joy of the Lord's appearing.

So, if those who die in Christ go straight to paradise and participate in the Rapture without the need of further cleansing, doesn't it make one better off to already be dead at the time Jesus returns for us?

A danger inherent with in the teaching of the partial-Rapture theory is that it makes one better off to be dead than alive when it happens. If a follower of Jesus is already with Him, he or she cannot miss out on the grand event. However, if a living disciple is not careful, he or she might miss out on the joy of the reunion and bear the great suffering of being left behind.

Is There an Advantage to Faithful Service?

If the Lord includes all believers in the Rapture, is there any advantage to walking with the Lord before He returns? Will our faithful service matter?

Absolutely!

First, Scripture tells us that our rewards will differ based on our faithful service to the Lord. In 1 Corinthians 3:11–15, Paul wrote about believers standing before the Judgment Seat of Christ:

> For no one can lay a foundation other than that which is laid, which is Jesus Christ. Now if anyone builds on the foundation with gold, silver, precious stones, wood, hay, straw—each one's work will become manifest, for the Day will disclose it, because it will be revealed by fire, and the fire will test what sort of work each one has done. If the work that anyone has built on the foundation survives, he will receive a reward. If anyone's work is burned up, he will suffer loss, though he himself will be saved, but only as through fire.

Although as believers we cannot miss out on the Rapture, the extent of our faithful service for Jesus will make a difference when we at last stand before our Savior. Those who have been careless in their walk with the Lord will miss out on rewards at that time.

Second, there's a special blessing reserved for those watching for the Lord's return. Second Timothy 4:8 says that those who love Jesus' "appearing" receive a "crown of righteousness." This signifies that those who eagerly await His return will receive special recognition. Jesus will approvingly acknowledge our watchfulness during these last days.

Summary

Scripture *never* distinguishes between believers included in the Rapture and those who will miss it—never. In 1 Thessalonians 4:13–5:11 and in 1 Corinthians 15:50–56, the Apostle Paul provides lengthy discussions of the Lord's appearing for His Church. Nowhere in these passages do we find even a hint of separation between believers who are ready versus those who are not. If anything, we see precisely the opposite: the inclusion of *all* those in Christ, whether dead or alive, in the Rapture.

When the Lord returns, it will be much better for believers walking with the Lord than for those engaged in sin or living solely for the things of this world. Those watching for His appearing will also receive a special crown.

Notes

1. Randy Alcorn, *Heaven* (Carol Stream, IL: Tyndale House, 2004), p. 26.
2. Alcorn, p. 410.
3. Paul David Tripp, *New Morning Mercies—A Daily Gospel Devotional* (Wheaton, IL: Crossway, 2014), January 21 (the book does not have page numbers, just dates).
4. John Eldredge, *All Things New* (Nashville, TN: Nelson Books, 2017), pp. 220–21.
5. J. I. Packer, *Hot Tub Religion* (Wheaton, IL: Tyndale House Publishers, 1987) p. 88.
6. Ibid., p. 95.
7. Tripp, *New Morning Mercies*, June 7.
8. Tripp, March 11.
9. Ola Elizabeth Winslow, *Jonathan Edwards: Basic Writings* (New York: New American Library, 1966), p. 142.
10. Erich Sauer, *The Triumph of the Crucified* (Wm. B. Eerdmans Publishing Company, Grand Rapids, MI, 1952), p. 150.
11. Quote from a sermon by Amir Tsarfati speaking at Calvary Chapel Church in Kaneohe, Hawaii, August 7, 2016.
12. Charles L Feinberg, *God Remembers* (American Board of Missions to the Jews, Inc., New York, 1965), p. 235.
13. J. Dwight Pentecost, *Things to Come* (Grand Rapids, MI: Zondervan, 1958), p. 93.

14. David Limbaugh, *The Emmaus Code* (Washington, DC: Regency, 2015) p. 106.
15. Ibid., p. 123.
16. Saucy, Robert L., *The Church in God's Program* (Chicago: Moody Press, 1972), pp. 80–81.
17. Grant R. Jeffrey, *Triumphant Return: The Coming Kingdom of God* (Colorado Springs, CO: Waterbrook Press, 2001), p. 148.
18. John F. Walvoord, *Daniel: The Key to Prophetic Revelation* (Chicago: Moody Press 1971), p. 161.
19. R. Laird Harris, *Theological Wordbook of the Old Testament, Volume 1* (Chicago: Moody Press, 1980), p. 949.
20. Alva J. McClain., *The Greatness of the Kingdom* (Winona Lake, IN: BMH Books, 1959), p. 21.
21. Allen, D. Matthew, *Theology Adrift: The Early Church Fathers and Their Views of Eschatology*, a paper published on the Bible.org website, chapter 2.
22. Philip Schaff, *History of the Christian Church, Vol. II* (Grand Rapids, MI: Eerdmans, 1910; reprinted 1995), p. 614.
23. Eusebius, "Ecclesiastical History," *Ante-Nicene Library*, Vol. 3 (Grand Rapids, MI: Eerdmans, 1987) p. 39.
24. Grant R. Jeffrey, *Triumphant Return: The Coming Kingdom of God* (Colorado Springs, CO: Waterbrook Press, 2001), p. 124.
25. Justin Martyr, "Dialogue with Trypho," *The Ante-Nicene Fathers,* 10 vols., Vol. 1 (Grand Rapids, MI: Eerdmans, 1979),, pp. 239–40.
26. Ibid., p. 560.
27. Jeffrey, *Triumphant Return,* p. 126.
28. Lactantius, *The Divine Institutes*, 7.24, *The Ante-Nicene Fathers*, vol. VII, p. 219.
29. Ibid.
30. Alcorn, *Heaven*, p. 477.
31. Ibid.
32. Ibid.
33. Ibid.
34. Thomas Williams, *Augustine and the Platonists*, a lecture given to the

Freshman Program of Christ College, the Honors College of Valparaiso University, October 23, 2003.
35. Allen, D. Matthew, *Theology Adrift: The Early Church Fathers and Their Views of Eschatology*, a paper published on the Bible.org website, chapter 5.
36. Ibid.
37. Bernard Ramm, *Protestant Biblical Interpretation* (Grand Rapids, MI: Baker Book House 1970), p. 58.
38. Dr. Andy Woods, *Ever Reforming* (Taos, NM: Dispensational Publishing House, 2018), p. 64.
39. William Watson, "The Rise of Philo-Semitism and Premillennialism During the Seventeenth and Eighteenth Centuries," Pre-Tribulation Research Center website, https://www.pre-trib.org/articles/all-articles.
40. Woods, *Ever Reforming*, p. 48.
41. Dr. Thomas Ice, "Amillennialism," *The Popular Encyclopedia of Bible Prophecy*, eds. Tim LaHaye and Ed Hindson (Eugene, OR: Harvest House, 2004), pp. 19–20.
42. McClain, *Greatness of the Kingdom*, p. 531.
43. Grant R. Jeffrey, *Triumphant Return: The Coming Kingdom of God* (Colorado Springs, CO: Waterbrook Press, 2001), p. 165.
44. John MacArthur, *The MacArthur New Testament Commentary—1 & 2 Thessalonians* (Chicago: Moody Press, 2002), p. 136.
45. John F. Walvoord, *The Blessed Hope and the Tribulation* (Grand Rapids, MI: Zondervan, 1969) p. 72.
46. Colin Brown, ed., *Dictionary of New Testament Theology Vol. 2*, (Grand Rapids, MI: Zondervan, 1969) p. 244.
47. Wayne A. Brindle, "Imminence," *The Popular Encyclopedia of Bible Prophecy*, eds. Tim LaHaye and Ed Hindson (Eugene, OR: Harvest House, 2004), p. 145.
48. Hiebert, D Edmond, *The Thessalonian Epistles* (Chicago: Moody Press, 1971), p. 189.
49. J. Dwight Pentecost, *Things to Come* (Grand Rapids, MI: Zondervan, 1958), p. 230.
50. Ibid.
51. Robert L. Thomas, *Lexical and Syntactical Exegesis, Synthesis, Solutions: I*

Thessalonians, Class notes from "Solutions to Selected Difficult Passages," 1973, p. 26.
52. John F. Walvoord, *The Rapture Question* (Grand Rapids, MI: Zondervan, 1979) p. 239
53. Hiebert, D Edmond, *The Thessalonian Epistles* (Chicago: Moody Press, 1971), p. 301.
54. Ibid., p. 302.
55. Andy Woods, *The Falling Away—Spiritual Departure or Physical Rapture?* (Taos, NM: Dispensational Publishing House, 2018), p. 43.
56. The Wycliffe Bible (1384), Tyndale Bible (1526), Coverdale Bible (1535), Cranmer Bible (1539), Breeches Bible (1576), Beza Bible (1583), and Geneva Bible (1608) all translated *apostasia* as a physical departure.
57. Andy Woods, *The Falling Away—Spiritual Departure or Physical Rapture?* (Taos, NM: Dispensational Publishing House, 2018), p. 19.
58. Ibid., p. 23.
59. Ibid., p. 16.
60. Cyprian, *Treatises of Cyprian*, "On the Mortality," section 25.
61. D. Edmond Hiebert, *The Thessalonian Epistles*, p. 313.
62. Ibid.
63. Thomas, p. 324. Also referenced by Dr. Thomas in regard to this is: Archibald T. Robertson, *A Grammar of the Greek New Testament in the Light of Historical Research* (Nashville, TN: Broadman Press, 1934), pp. 208–9.
64. Thomas Ice, "*Kept From the Hour" Website: https://www.pre-trib.org/articles/all-articles/message/kept-from-the-hour/read.*
65. Todd Hampson, *The Non-Prophet's Guide to the Book of Revelation* (Eugene, OR: Harvest House, 2019). p. 43.
66. Ibid., p. 44.
67. John MacArthur, *The MacArthur New Testament Commentary—Revelation 1–11* (Chicago: Moody Press, 1999), p. 149.
68. Thomas Ice, "Who Are the 24 Elders in Revelation?" Website: https://www.pre-trib.org/articles/all-articles/message/who-are-the-24-elders-in-revelation/read.
69. Randy Alcorn, *Heaven*, p. 172.
70. Carol Talbot, *For This I Was Born* (Chicago: Moody Press, 1977), p. 273.
71. Ibid.

72. Based on the movie *Before the Wrath*, which dramatizes the latest archeological findings of Galilean wedding customs in the first century AD.
73. Ibid.
74. Ibid.
75. Quote is from "The Rapture and the Jewish on the Wedding," Bridal Covenant website, http://www.bridalcovenant.com/wedding1.html.
76. *Before the Wrath.*
77. "Rapture and the Jewish on the Wedding."
78. John F. Walvoord, *The Blessed Hope and the Tribulation* (Grand Rapids, MI: Zondervan, 1969) p. 48.
79. Irenaeus, "Against Heresies," *The Ante-Nicene Fathers,* 10 vols., Vol. 1 (Grand Rapids, MI: Eerdmans, 1979), p. 558.
80. *The Shepherd of Hermas,* Transl. J. B. Lightfoot, Early Christian Writings website, vision 4. http://earlychristianwritings.com/shepherd.html.
81. Cyprian, *Treatises of Cyprian,* "On the Mortality," section 25.
82. Francis Gumerlock, "The Rapture in the Apocalypse of Elijah; in Bibliotheca Sacra 170 (Oct.–Dec. 2013), p. 420.
83. Jeffrey, *Triumphant Return,* p. 174.
84. Ibid., pp. 175–76.
85. Material on Dolcino comes from Francis Gumerlock, "A Rapture Citation in the Fourteenth Century," *Bibliotheca Sacra* (vol. 159, no. 635; July–September 2002), pp. 354–5.
86. Thomas Ice, "A History of Pre-Darby Rapture Advocates," Dec. 2011, article on the Pre-Trib Research Center, p. 7. https://www.pre-trib.org/articles/all-articles/message/a-history-of-pre-darby-rapture-advocates
87. Morgan Edwards, *Two Academical Exercises on Subjects Bearing the Following Titles; Millennium, Last-Novelties* (Philadelphia: Dobson and Lang, 1788), p. 7.
88. Ice, A *History of Pre-Darby Rapture Advocates.*
89. Tim LaHaye, "Pretribulationism," *The Popular Encyclopedia of Bible Prophecy* eds. Tim LaHaye and Ed Hindson (Eugene, OR: Harvest House, 2004), p290.
90. The movie, *Before the Wrath,* depicts how these customs point to a pre-Tribulation Rapture.
91. Randy Alcorn, *Heaven,* p. 124.
92. Eldredge, *All Things New,* pp. 93–94.

93. Wikipedia, "Imagine" (John Lennon song).
94. Grant R. Jeffrey, *Armageddon—Appointment with Destiny* (Toronto: Frontier Research Publications, 1997), p. 228.
95. Alva J. McClain., *The Greatness of the Kingdom* (Winona Lake, IN: BMH Books, 1959), p. 531.
96. Words from the Christian song, "In Christ Alone," written by Keith Getty and Stuart Townsend.
97. Alcorn, *Heaven*, p. 472.
98. John Eldredge, *Desire* (Nashville, TN: Thomas Nelson, 2007), p.110.
99. Ibid. pp. 110–111
100. Ibid. p. 119.
101. Alcorn, *Heaven*, p. 187.
102. Ibid., p. 253.
103. Ibid., p. 269.
104. Snobele, Stephen D., *Statement on the date 2060, March 2003; updated May 2003 and June2003.* Taken from a website titled "Isaac Newton Theology, Prophecy, Science and Religion," https://isaac-newton.org/statement-on-the-date-2060/.
105. My information on the temple preparations comes from following the Temple Institute on Facebook for *several* years (https://www.facebook.com/templeinstitute). The Temple Institute is a nonprofit Jewish organization dedicated to rebuilding the Temple in Jerusalem.
106. Peter Koenig, *The Global Reset—Unplugged.* "The Deep State," on Global Research website, https://www.globalresearch.ca/global-reset-unplugged/5716178 July 24, 2020.
107. Quote from the WEF website: https://www.weforum.org/focus/the-great-reset.
108. Peter Koenig, *The Twilight Zone: Covid, the World Economic Forum (WEF) and Eugenics*, February 19, 2021, https://www.globalresearch.ca/the-twilight-zone-covid-the-world-economic-forum-wef-and-eugenics/5737778.
109. https://rumble.com/vemuo5-sunday-night-live-with-tom-hughes.html. Note: This video was originally on YouTube, but likely was censored and removed.